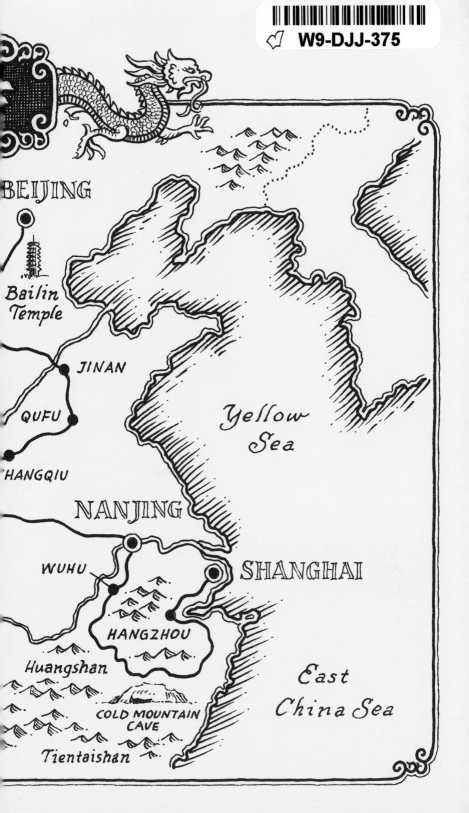

BEIJING

Bailin
Temple

JINAN

QUFU

ZHANGQIU

NANJING

WUHU

SHANGHAI

HANGZHOU

Huangshan

COLD MOUNTAIN
CAVE

Tientaishan

Yellow
Sea

East
China Sea

SEEKING
THE CAVE

SEEKING
THE CAVE

A PILGRIMAGE
TO COLD MOUNTAIN

James P. Lenfestey

MILKWEED EDITIONS

Published 2014 by Milkweed Editions
Printed in the United States of America
Cover design by Mary Austin Speaker
Cover artwork by Brice Marden
Author photo by Larry Marcus
Endpaper map by Chris Costello
14 15 16 17 18 5 4 3 2 1
First Edition

Milkweed Editions, an independent nonprofit publisher, gratefully acknowledges sustain-
ing support from the Bush Foundation; the Jerome Foundation; the Lindquist & Vennum
Foundation; the McKnight Foundation; the National Endowment for the Arts; the Target
Foundation; and other generous contributions from foundations, corporations, and individu-
als. Also, this activity is made possible by the voters of Minnesota through a Minnesota State
Arts Board Operating Support grant, thanks to a legislative appropriation from the arts and
cultural heritage fund, and a grant from the Wells Fargo Foundation Minnesota. For a full
listing of Milkweed Editions supporters, please visit www.milkweed.org.

Library of Congress Cataloging-in-Publication Data

Lenfestey, James P.
  Seeking the cave : a pilgrimage to Cold Mountain / James P. Lenfestey.
    pages cm
  ISBN 978-1-57131-346-1 (hardback) -- ISBN 978-1-57131-897-8
(ebook)
  1. Lenfestey, James P.--Travels--China. 2. Authors, American--21st
century--Biography. 3. China--Description and travel. I. Title.
  PS3612.E528Z46 2014
  811'.6--dc23
  [B]
                                        2014004199

Milkweed Editions is committed to ecological stewardship. We strive to align our book
production practices with this principle, and to reduce the impact of our operations in
the environment. We are a member of the Green Press Initiative, a nonprofit coalition of
publishers, manufacturers, and authors working to protect the world's endangered forests
and conserve natural resources. *Seeking the Cave* was printed on acid-free 100%
postconsumer-waste paper by Edwards Brothers Malloy.

To Cold Mountain

and

Burton Watson, who gave me the gift

of Cold Mountain's songs;

Bill Porter, who took me there;

Margaret, Mike, and Ed,

boon companions on the journey.

CONTENTS

PREFACE:
Han-Shan Haibun   xiii

PROLOGUE:
My Own Private China   xvii

BOOK I
FINDING THE PATH

ONE On the Road   3

TWO Between Two Hurricanes   9

THREE Encounter with the Arch-Translator   15

FOUR Passage to More than Kyoto   23

FIVE Kyoto Koan   27

SIX Rendezvous at Narita   33

SEVEN Beijing: The Biggest Bell in the World   39

EIGHT In Xanadu Did Genghis Khan   45

NINE Jia Dao and the Riddle of Sound and Sense   51

BOOK II
FROM BUDDHIST TEMPLES TO SOARING CRANES

TEN Buddhists for the Night   59

ELEVEN Breakfast with Confucius   65

TWELVE Speedways, Corn Roads, and Apple Lanes   71

THIRTEEN Ordinary and Extraordinary Graves 79

FOURTEEN Du Fu's Sorrow 85

FIFTEEN Bai Juyi's "Idle Droning" 93

SIXTEEN What the Old Master Wrote 97

SEVENTEEN The Soaring Cranes of Xi'an 101

EIGHTEEN Road to Heaven 105

NINETEEN First Adventure in Hermit Hunting 109

TWENTY An Evening with Dr. Hu 115

TWENTY-ONE Turtles All the Way Down 123

BOOK III
SLEEPLESS DREAMS TO DREAMLESS SLEEP

TWENTY-TWO Give It Its True Name 129

TWENTY-THREE Moon Music 133

TWENTY-FOUR Drinking Wine with Li Bai 137

TWENTY-FIVE Two Depressing Poems in Wuhu 141

TWENTY-SIX Beginning-to-Believe Peak 145

TWENTY-SEVEN The Floating World of Poet-Engineers 151

TWENTY-EIGHT "Six" and the Single Traveler 157

TWENTY-NINE Cold Mountain: Whose Story Is It? 161

THIRTY The Hermit of Cold Mountain 165

THIRTY-ONE "The Birds and Their Chatter" 171

THIRTY-TWO The Nun's Priest's Tale 183

THIRTY-THREE One New God 187

THIRTY-FOUR Meanwhile, Back in the Ka-ching 189

EPILOGUE:

Christmas Morning 193

POSTSCRIPT:

Finding My Own True Name 195

APPENDIX:

Endnotes; Coda; Permissions; List of Sources; Acknowledgments 199

Then do folk long to go on pilgrimage,
And palmers to go seeking out strange strands,
To distant shrines well known in sundry lands.

CHAUCER, PROLOGUE,
THE CANTERBURY TALES

There is only one way to travel and that is inward.

JANE HIRSHFIELD

PREFACE

Han-Shan Haibun

*It is of the highest urgency for the creative artist to be
honestly attentive to the sources of his inspiration and
to the obligation those sources impose.*

FRED GOSS AND JAMES BOGAN

SPARKS OF FIRE: BLAKE IN A NEW AGE

In the fall of 2006 I traveled to Japan and China seeking
the cave of Han-shan, Cold Mountain, a recluse whose
poems I have loved for more than thirty years, who took
his final name from the place where he lived. I returned
with notebooks filled with impressions and poems. Simple
enough, I thought, to add back the skeleton and musculature of
narration over the beating heart of the poems. In practice, the
haibun process pushed me to immerse myself not only in my journals but also in additional studies of Chinese poetry and poets,
the Japanese *haibun* form itself, and, to my surprise, memory.

Beginning in my mid-fifties, a new feeling began to grow
inside me, a surprisingly powerful urge I came to term "seeking the cave." I felt an increasing pull toward quietude if not
solitude, toward the stillness of dawn and away from evening
enthusiasms, toward contemplation and away from engagement.
My pilgrimage to Cold Mountain cave, raucous as it sometimes

was through the noisy, neon-lit frame of modern China—what we quickly dubbed the "Ka-ching Dynasty" for its obsession with the gleam and rattle of money—pays homage to that pull I eventually could not resist. My pilgrimage to Cold Mountain, the poet and the place, is its metaphor.

I present myself as no expert on any of this—neither China nor Chinese poetry nor translation nor pilgrimage nor *haibun*. I am only a man trying to find the best means to tell the story of an American life that mysteriously resonates with the poems and poetic style of a poet who lived, if he lived at all and isn't a literary fiction, in a cave somewhere in the Tientai Mountains of China 1,200 years ago. In seeking the actual cave to which the poet Cold Mountain is believed to have retired, and from which he wrote his poems and took his final name, I was seeking—it's clear to me now—my own true name. Perhaps these scribblings from the notebooks of my travels, some refined into poems—all refined after acute critical readings by Gary Snyder, John Rosenwald, Eric Utne, Thomas R. Smith, J. P. White, traveling companions Mike Hazard, Margaret Telfer and Ed McConaghay, and editor Daniel Slager—will resonate with the reader's own voyages external and internal. Perhaps you too will learn your own true name for how to live within the wonderings of the last decades of a life. Special thanks to the Anderson Center for residencies that allowed me the time to complete this manuscript.

JAMES P. LENFESTEY

Mackinac Island, Michigan, after finishing at dawn
The Narrow Road to the Deep North and Other Travel Sketches
by Matsuo Bashō, translated by Nobuyuki Yuasa.

A NOTE ON SPELLING

Chinese characters have been transliterated into the Roman alphabet using many different systems. Until recently the Wade-Giles system was most prominent, through which many English readers came to know Li Po, Tu Fu, Po Chü-i, and Su T'ung-p'o, for example. The latest writing system, called Pinyin, seems more closely to approximate modern Mandarin pronunciation, e.g., Li Bai, Du Fu, Bai Juyi, and Su Dongpo, and is the spelling system I have generally employed. In China if I mentioned Li Po or Tu Fu I got no reaction, but if I said Li Bai or Du Fu faces brightened, like meeting old friends. Few brightened at the mention of Han-shan, little read in China and not taught in school. One spelling exception is the name of the mountain region Han-shan called home: "Tiantai" in Pinyin. I missed the sound of the soft *e*, the way I imagined the sound of "Tientai," so I have maintained that spelling.

My Own Private China

Do you remember that cliff
We once imagined—hundreds of swallow holes,
And an old Chinese poem rolled up inside
Each hole! We can't unroll them here. We have
To climb inside.

ROBERT BLY,

"LETTER TO JAMES WRIGHT"

In 1974 Charlie Miller, proprietor of the World Eye Bookshop in Greenfield, Massachusetts, placed into my hand *Cold Mountain: 100 Poems by T'ang Poet Han-shan*, translated by Burton Watson. "Try these," he said, like a doctor prescribing medicine to a patient.

At the time I was director of a nearby alternative high school that spilled its special brand of chaos over the Connecticut River Valley nearby. I often came to his bookstore, a source of delight and solace for me. A poet himself, and friend of Auden, Charlie had become a good enough friend of mine that he could sense what I needed.

I read Cold Mountain no. 10:

Here we languish, a bunch of poor scholars,
Battered by extremes of hunger and cold.
Out of work, our only joy is poetry:

Scribble, scribble, we wear out our brains.
Who will read the works of such men?
On that point you can save your sighs.
We could inscribe our poems on biscuits
And the homeless dogs wouldn't deign to nibble.

For the first time in my life, I laughed out loud at a poem!
What a joyful relief to hear expressed the mad futility of
poets who scribbled out poems night after night as I did.
Soon enough I swallowed Han-shan's other short poems like
aspirin. His commonplace language, brusque truths, satiric
jabs at bureaucracy, and longing for quiet mind entered me
unmediated by any teacher, seeming to salve wounds I didn't
know I had. I fell in love with that voice, like that of an older
brother I never knew, and for the first and only time in my
life began to "write back" to an author, scratching spontane-
ous responses in the margins of Watson's volume.

Homeless Dogs

I languish in a car with battered friends,
the world the same as before we tried to fix it.
Young people won't listen to us, and old ones
mock our shaggy hair.
In despair, we read Han-shan's poems as we drive.
Those scribed on stones make us laugh.
Those carved on trees make us cry.
We devour these thousand-year-old biscuits
like homeless dogs!

My hungry poetry dog had found its bark.

Soon enough, my wife, three children, and I moved to Minneapolis and rebooted our lives. We dove deep into community, schools, and politics while I started an environmental business, then went into marketing communications, finally joining the *Star Tribune* editorial board, and the great questions of life were, for the nonce, settled. Yet all the while I continued to "write back" to my mysterious poet friend, first late at night and then, when the children stayed up later than I could, early in the morning, following a voice that never stopped thrilling me.

Beginning sometime in my mid-fifties, I developed a dream, a fantasy really, I came to call "seeking the cave." I'd see myself wandering the back country of China, seeking the actual cave of Cold Mountain, a poet who may never have existed and who, if he did, is said to have disappeared into a crack in a mountain. And all I wanted to do was say "thank you."

Madness.

And yet, in the fall of 2006, at age sixty-two, there I was, climbing a stone stairway from the dusty trail below toward the open mouth of Cold Mountain cave.

Madness indeed.

Men ask the way to Cold Mountain
Cold Mountain: there's no through trail

This is the poet's journey. In my case the trail was long, and included many of the necessary joys and sorrows of a relatively educated, literate, fortunate American life. Now married forty years, a grandfather, retired teacher/ad man/journalist, and poet since a boy, I saw the clouds of a busy life part just long enough that I thought I could perceive the trail ahead. And so I stepped out.

The summer before the scheduled mid-September departure, there arrived storms of trouble and confusion and doubt about this idea. One night, up alone, I heard a cricket singing outside the summer cabin door. I had never heard one there before in twenty years. I rose and went to the screen door and gently pulled it open. There he was, in his dark monk's robe, knocking to come in. I took him in my palm. He had a song for me.

SEEKING
THE CAVE

BOOK I

FINDING THE PATH

CHAPTER ONE

ON THE ROAD

September 19, 2006

I hugged my wife good-bye at the Charles Lindbergh terminal in Minneapolis, tears burning my eyes. My eyes streamed again, this time with laughter, as I left phone messages for our four children, making certain they understood that if I disappeared into a crack in the mountain, as Han-shan had done, they could be confident of my love for each of them, if not my reliability as a father and grandfather.

The 747-400, Northwest flight 19 to Tokyo-Narita, was big as a movie theater. My traveling companion, videographer Mike Hazard, exulted over the empty seat between us, a gift from the airline gods, given the upcoming nine-hour flight and thirteen-hour time-zone shift, a body and mind bender common for business travelers but new to us.

We reviewed our plans. We would interview esteemed translator Burton Watson in Tokyo day after tomorrow, then visit Kyoto's Zen temples. Back at Narita Airport, we would meet traveling companions Margaret Telfer and Ed McConaghay and fly together to Beijing to meet our guide,

Bill Porter, the American Buddhist translator known as Red Pine. We would follow him for three weeks through the literary backcountry of China, ending, if all went well, at Cold Mountain cave. "It is a good thing we are doing," Mike said.

I could not believe I was finally on Cold Mountain's trail. My uncanny wife had whispered into my ear at departure, "It's as if you are in love with someone else." I tried to remember how it happened.

Here's what I knew. Of the nearly three hundred poems attributed to Han-shan, Watson had translated only those he found rich in human content. As important, he had used evidence within the poems to give them a chronological order, which revealed, he said, "a chronicle of spiritual search." Clearly I was on some search as well. But for what?

That Boy Needs a Book in his Hands

When the portrait painter took up her brush to capture me
  at three,
she told my mother: "That boy needs a book in his hands."
She made my eyes big, a lie. But my hands did not lie.
The radar of my palms flies me through insect nights.
Fingertips sense syllables carved on rocks and trees.
I have heard the dull thud of fists greeting other skulls.
My open hand rebels, curved like an ear, a turtle's shell,
a woman's body, a child's head of hair, the earth itself.

Since boyhood, I had been unable to stop my pen from scratching out poems. I wrote poetic essays in high school instead of academic prose. At Dartmouth College, while preparing to be an engineer, my family's concrete dream, I studied poetry with Tony Herbold. In graduate school at the University of Wisconsin, while studying eighteenth-century English literature, I read poetry with James Merrill. In my free time I sought out Robert Bly's revolutionary little magazine, *The Fifties* and *The Sixties*, in the rare-book vault at the university. I loved the fresh voices from around the world I found there, as well as Bly's spirited criticism of stuffy academic and political discourse, and his treatment of poems not as intellectual baubles but as prophetic, healing texts.

Married three months after college graduation, three weeks after my twenty-second birthday, the day after Susan's twentieth, we roared off pell-mell into graduate school, teaching, and parenthood. Our first child was born the following year, then another, then another. Ten years later Dora was born, Greek for "gift." In those hectic, love-saturated decades, I wrote poetry at night like a thief.

The poems piled up like fallen leaves.

Now, taking off above the clouds of a full and busy life, I held in my hand a book of my own poems, twenty-one short responses to Cold Mountain's call. I had set the lead type myself one letter at a time, upside down and backward, a hermetic, meditative task. The delicate Japanese paper fluttered like butterflies' wings. Publisher Scott King had hand-sewn the printed sheets together into a stab binding echoing the books of ancient China. Dan Garner had contributed a woodcut of Cold Mountain, the necklace of prayer beads alone taking him hours to carve. The result was something that felt simultaneously new and old, heavy and light, a gift that could finally express my gratitude to Cold Mountain and his translator, Burton Watson, to whom it was dedicated:

To Burton Watson,
whose musical translations helped me hear Han-shan's songs.

In my backpack I carried a clutch of other books, necessities new and old:

- My worn 1974 copy of Watson's *Cold Mountain*, my ecstatic responses chicken-scratched over the margins—a sacred text to me.
- Bill Porter's *The Collected Songs of Cold Mountain*, whose photograph of Cold Mountain cave had launched this journey, and his newest translation project, *Poems of the Masters: China's Classic Anthology of T'ang and Sung Dynasty Verse*, both bilingual editions.
- *The Columbia Book of Chinese Poetry: From Early Times to the Thirteenth Century*, translated and edited by Watson, a volume familiar to any American student of Chinese literature but new to me.
- Sam Hamill and J. P. Seaton's handsome little red book, *The Poetry of Zen*, published by Shambhala in 2004, signed to me by Sam in 2005 at a reading in Northfield, Minnesota.
- *Ryōkan: Zen Monk-Poet of Japan*, Watson's translations of a poet-eccentric (1758–1831) who also claimed Cold Mountain as his teacher.
- *A Field Guide to the Birds of China*, a brick of a book ordered for the trip.
- Two journals, their lined pages empty and waiting.

Pressed into the seatback at takeoff, I opened *The Columbia Book of Chinese Poetry* as Minnesota's lakes disappeared below me like fallen silver coins. "The Chinese have customarily looked upon poetry as the chief glory of their literary tradition," Watson wrote. I relaxed into that revelation just as the plane's video terminals unspooled an episode of *Everybody Loves Raymond*, a chief glory of the modern American literary tradition. I fell asleep reading a rueful poem written in the first century BCE by Lady Pan, once Emperor Ch'eng's favorite concubine, now slighted for another:

> I reflect that man, born into this world,
> passes as swiftly as though floating on a stream.
> Already I've known fame and eminence,
> the finest gifts the living can enjoy.
> I will strive to please my spirit, taste every delight,
> since true happiness cannot be counted on.

CHAPTER TWO

BETWEEN TWO HURRICANES

September 19, 2006,
5,953 miles from home

Flight 19 landed at Tokyo's Narita Airport at 4:30 p.m. local time. The afternoon temperature of eighty-one degrees and the soaking humidity surprised two Minnesota men. Mike and I immediately lost each other at the massive airport, realizing, on our chance reunion, that with no cell phones or backup plan for finding each other, we'd better stick together.

On the bus to our downtown hotel, we struck up an English conversation with a seatmate, affable Mr. Goto, a forty-year-old businessman wearing a conservative dark suit under long hair and funky rectangular glasses. He told us that he lived in Santiago, Chile, where he exported tankers full of wine to Japan.

I laughed at the intoxicating image of a tanker full of wine. Goto laughed too, and cheerfully volunteered to be our tour guide in Tokyo. After Mike and I checked into our hotel, Goto walked us to the famous Ginza, like Times Square on neon amphetamines, the flashing heart of Japan's global electronics empire. Although it represented everything I'd hoped to leave behind, Mike and I gaped slack-jawed like every other tourist. We continued on to traditional Yakitori Street, located beside the Yūrakuchō train station, where we grabbed a barrel-top table at one of the minuscule sidewalk cafés. We devoured a brace of delicious *yakitori*, invented here—skewers of chicken grilled with different spices—plus a plate of pickled onions and mugs of cold draft Sapporo. Then we drifted back to our hotel.

I awoke at 5:00 a.m. to an unfamiliar sound from the bathroom, Mike's electric razor. By six we were wandering the narrow corridors of the massive Tokyo fish market, which a friend insisted should be our first stop. We watched auction-eers chant over torpedo-sized frozen tuna covered in a skin of frost. Large plastic vats squirmed with eels and pulsed with sea urchins, their spines removed and pulsing in sepa-rate vats. Dockworkers in orange jumpsuits forklifted squeaky Styrofoam boxes of sea life onto motorized carts that rattled toward a cordon of idling delivery trucks. The scene throbbed with life, but I felt a rush of despair for the silent sea nearby.

At the Tokyo Fish Market, 6:00 a.m.

Someone invented language for this—
to dedicate the prows of sleek steel trawlers,
to name these frozen bodies *tuna*, not *torpedoes*,
to name their tongues *tongues*, still black and hungry,
samurai nature unable to resist the proffered hook.
Every word living in the sea is sold here.
In the quiet bay beneath the bridge, a lone cormorant
   dives free.
Still, I cannot help but feel the voice of the sea is lost.

A cab scooted us to Takashimaya Department Store before nine, as a friend had advised us we must not miss the store's opening spectacle—white-gloved salesgirls singing the corporate song. The store opened at ten, so we waited on the busy street outside like scruffy American mannequins as workers rushed by to their offices.

IN FRONT OF TAKASHIMAYA DEPARTMENT
STORE BEFORE IT OPENS
Listen to the shoe soles, like herds of gazelles!
Tap slap, tap slap of backless heels,
woodblock prints of sandal flats,
leather swish of knee-high boots,
oxford scrape of company men.
All march to the tune of shiny dark towers.
Across the street, the tallest crane in Japan
pivots against the sky, and flies higher.

Catching a badly needed espresso at Tully's Coffee across the street, we managed to miss the opening ceremony. Still, when we entered the store, lovely blue-suited women bowed to us. *"Ohayou gozaimasu."* Everywhere, more bows. We slipped down to the celebrated basement food court and feasted on free samples: pear sauce on bread, steamed moon cakes filled with sweet miso or red bean paste, a delicious sweet and vinegar cabbage, a taste of earthy Argentinean Malbec, perhaps from Goto's tanker. A white-gloved elevator attendant whisked us to the rooftop garden, where a small boy and his mother delighted at a butterfly basking in raindrops from the spray of the elderly gardener's hose. What a delicious way to alight in a new country, I thought.

A Butterfly Visits the Roof Garden at Takashimaya

The gardener sprays roof grass with rainbows,
hose arcing back and forth across his bent frame.
A butterfly trembles beneath silver drops,
wings inset with turquoise glistening in sunlit prayer.
Like the cicadas who called all night in this ancient city
paved over rubble of the last Great War, surprises emerge.
How did he get here? the delighted child wants to know.
The butterfly? The gardener? Me?

The boy's bored mother introduced herself to Mike and me in excellent English. Daughter of a diplomat, she was raised around the world, married now to a Japanese business-man. She badly missed the freedom and individuality she found overseas. "In Japan, you feel . . . I don't know. I like to be different. I *am* different, but here it is very hard. Everyone wears the same black—I want to wear bright colors. You going to Kabuki? I drive you to Kabuki. I have German car. I like to drive fast. My husband is okay, he travels a lot. That's okay too. This is my only child in sixteen years. I like being a mother. I have so much sympathy for the princess. She is trapped. Nothing she can do."

At the famous Kabuki Theater, Mike and I bought two bento boxes for carry-in lunch and tickets for the cheap fourth-floor balcony. The actors' painted faces and stylized drama fascinated us for an hour or so until we fell asleep from jet lag fatigue.

Back at the hotel I called Burton Watson at the phone number he'd sent me, and we arranged our interview for mid-morning the next day. He did not want to meet at his apart-ment—"Too small, too far away," he said—so he would meet us in the hotel lobby. Mike and I spent the rest of the day madly scouting nearby parks, cemeteries, museums, and temples for an elegant interview location. In the end, we set-tled on Mike's least favorite option, our hotel room, the only suitably quiet place we could find in this noisy, crowded city.

At 5:20 a.m. the phone rang. It was Goto, his body restless with the same jet lag as ours, offering to take us to see the fish market. I told him we'd done that already, so he offered to take us to breakfast. I thanked him for his generous hospitality, and the enduring image of a cargo ship filled with wine, but today we must begin our trek on the path to Cold Mountain. As we signed off, not to see each other again, I mentioned my surprise at the intense humidity in Tokyo. "This is the best weather of the autumn season," Goto answered. "Before you arrive, a hur-ricane. After you go, a hurricane. You have landed between two hurricanes. The gods are on your side."

CHAPTER THREE

ENCOUNTER WITH THE
ARCH-TRANSLATOR

After breakfast, Mike tested his cameras while I ordered an extra cup of tea. Mike was prepared. I was not. As a newspaper editorial writer for a decade, I had routinely interviewed major business, scientific, and political leaders without the slightest trepidation. But this was Dr. Burton Watson, preeminent translator and scholar who, at eighty years old, still produced elegant texts! What enduring work had I ever really done? Yes, I was in love with the sound and rhythm of Watson's translations, but I understood little of China, Japan, Buddhism, or, really, of poetry, though I was helplessly seized in its grasp much of my life.

I paced the hotel lobby. Right on time, a slight American pushed slowly through the revolving entrance door. He was lightly stooped, bald with a large mole decorating his forehead, wearing black heavy-framed 1950s-style glasses. He had warm, watery brown eyes, full lips, and the soft, gentle voice of a shy man. I awkwardly shook his hand (I had imagined a bear hug!), and gingerly ushered him into the elevator to our room. After introducing him to Mike, I prepared three cups of green tea while Mike seated him in the corner chair and arranged the lapel microphone.

There were surprises all around. I showed him my cherished edition of his *Cold Mountain*, my responses chicken-scratched all over the margins. He showed us his two-volume manuscript of Cold Mountain's poems, woodblock-printed in 1756, that he had purchased in 1956 at a bookstall in Kyoto. Stab-bound like my book dedicated to him, it held 303 poems, the vast majority attributed to Han-shan, the rest to his two friends, the Buddhist monk Feng-kan (Big Stick) and the foundling temple kitchenboy Shih-te (Pickup). The text was surrounded by extensive commentaries by Japanese Buddhist monks, who admired the eccentric and unpredictable Cold Mountain far more than Chinese Buddhist or Confucian scholars ever did.

He told us he fell in love with Chinese characters as a boy taking his parents' shirts to the neighborhood Chinese laundry in suburban New York, fascinated by the mysterious written forms. He joined the navy at seventeen before finishing high school, and while stationed in Yokohama harbor in 1943 made many trips into that devastated city. After graduation from the Chinese program at Columbia on the GI Bill, he immediately booked ship's passage back to Japan, seeking to get as close to China as the Cold War would allow. He landed in Japan in 1951, the occupation still under way. "Really," he said, "American missionaries were the only non-military people supposed to be there, but somehow I came as a teacher of English to Kyoto." He had left Japan infrequently ever since, including for a stint on the faculty at Columbia, which he fled when they wanted him to chair the department.

After finishing his PhD back at Columbia, he returned to Japan, part of the small expatriate community in Kyoto in the 1950s that included the poets Gary Snyder and Cid Corman, and Ruth Fuller Sasaki, the pioneering American Zen practitioner who later became a priest. Unknown to Watson at the time, Snyder had already translated twenty-four of Han-shan's poems as a graduate student at Berkeley (later published in *Evergreen Review* and in book form in *Riprap and Cold Mountain Poems*).

A beginning poet himself in those days, Watson told us translating Han-shan's poems became his first substantial undertaking. Watson worked for a time for Mrs. Sasaki at the First Zen Institute in Kyoto. When she read Arthur Waley's translations of twenty Cold Mountain poems in *Encounter* in 1954, she asked Watson to seek out the originals.

Cid Corman readily agreed to help edit Watson's early efforts at translation. "Cut this out, cut that out, this isn't doing anything . . . get rid of the verbiage," a confident Corman insisted to Watson's amazement, as Corman knew no Chinese (nor Japanese!). But Watson felt his advice sound and edited accordingly.

Watson trusted Corman, I guessed, because Corman was a poet. Watson said he still tries to keep his ear attuned to American English by reading contemporary poetry. I asked him to read out loud to us some of his Cold Mountain translations. In doing so, his voice dropped into a deeply moving poetic cadence. "I should have known!" I exclaimed to myself. "He has a poet's ear, that reverence for rhythm and sound. That explains the exceptional music of his translations."

In describing his translation technique, Watson confirmed that thought. "I know what the Chinese character means and implies and so on," he said. "And I can't just make up some other thing. On the other hand, I have a certain amount of leeway. It's what translators always say: because I've lost so much in other places, I should be allowed to make it up in places where I can . . . make it a little better than the original. So within those limits, I try to get the best language, the most vivid, effective—and the sound, of course, I'm always thinking of the sound. Some people apparently don't pay much attention to the sound."

He said he followed the Chinese form rigorously as well. "If it's an eight-line poem I come out with an eight-line translation. Because the lineation is very pronounced in the Chinese. Now [Kenneth] Rexroth didn't like that, so he runs it over into the next line. And [David] Hinton does the same, because he admires Rexroth. But the Chinese is so strong that it forces it on the English. . . . If you are going to use enjambment you have to enjamb every next line. I don't know why Rexroth did that. He didn't like end-stopped lines, but the Chinese form is very strong."

I told him about the diplomat's daughter at Takashimaya, who felt a tremendous conflict between the individuality she'd learned in the West and the conformity she felt living here. I wondered if that difference was part of the ungovernable Han-shan's charm to America's open-road ear? I remembered that Jack Kerouac wrote the novel *The Dharma Bums* after he and Allen Ginsberg visited Gary Snyder in Mill Valley, where Snyder was translating Han-shan for his

Berkeley professor. America's road scholar dedicated that book "to Han-shan."

Watson confided that at a family gathering back in the States after his father's death, he chose as a text a Han-shan poem. I asked him to read it to us.

COLD MOUNTAIN NO. 85
I came once to sit on Cold Mountain
And lingered here for thirty years.
Yesterday I went to see relatives and friends;
Over half had gone to the Yellow Springs.*
Bit by bit life fades like a guttering lamp,
Passes on like a river that never rests.
This morning I face my lonely shadow
And before I know it tears stream down.

Watson's eyes welled with tears as he recalled that gathering. Watson too had come to "sit" briefly in Japan and had "lingered" nearly forty years. Now he only rarely visited the States, and had visited mainland China only once. Although he had approached Tientai near Cold Mountain's cave, he had never reached it.

I asked him to read that poem one more time, but he answered, "Maybe it's too teary a note to end on." Instead he recited the final quatrain of his own response to Cold Mountain:

---

* According to ancient Chinese mythology (eighth century BCE) the Yellow Springs were an underground realm where the soul went after it left the body.

Do you have the poems of Han-shan in your house?
They're better for you than sutra-reading!
Write them out and paste them on a screen
where you can glance them over from time to time.

We laughed. "I do have the poems of Han-shan in my house," I said, "and have glanced them over for thirty years, thanks to you." "Take them along when you go on a picnic," he joked. "I do!" I answered. "I gave my son his own copy of your *Cold Mountain* on a picnic. Now he loves Han-shan through me, as I do through you." "He's fun to play with," Watson laughed.

After three hours that felt like three minutes, Mike finally unwound the microphone. I glanced at our cups of tea, cold and forgotten. Watson returned his treasured Han-shan to his travel bag and we left the hotel to stroll the grounds of nearby Zojoji Temple, Tokyo's cathedral of ritual Buddhism.

Wandering the manicured temple grounds, Watson explained his own Buddhist practice, the much quieter discipline of the Rinzai school of Zen. His master would assign him a koan—a famously enigmatic question or assertion—which he had to puzzle out through meditation. Sometimes the master approved his response right away. Sometimes approval took days or even years. He liked that practice, filled with disciplined probing of the mysterious nature of language and thought, letting go of the rational order of the world. "Zen says if you are happy, be happy, if you are sad, be sad. But don't hang on. Be where you are."

In the cemetery behind the temple, Watson explained the Japanese ceremony of death. Families placed the ashes of family

SEEKING THE CAVE

members at densely packed vertical grave markers, and ritually honored them by bringing water, flowers, and other beloved objects. "If he smoked cigarettes, they might leave a cigarette. It is too expensive for most families to be buried in Tokyo these days, so they go to cemeteries outside the city. There are also cemeteries for those without any relatives to care for them." He looked up. "That is where I will go," he said.

Watson declined our offer of lunch, and so, reluctantly, we left him at the Zojoji subway entrance. He waved good-bye and slowly disappeared down the steps, entering the mouth of the cave called Tokyo, his adopted home, his Cold Mountain.

THE ZOJOJI TEMPLE GATE—the original, constructed in 1613—is engraved with text translated on a nearby plaque: "Gate for getting delivered from earthly states of mind: greed, anger, and stupidity." Burton Watson passed through that gate many years ago, I thought. Much stupidity remained ahead for me, and probably greed and anger too. But my visit with him felt like an important step to begin to shed the husk of this world, like the cicadas whose freshly minted bodies sang throughout the long Tokyo night.

Bashō said:

Nothing in the cry
of cicadas suggests they
are about to die

(translated by Sam Hamill)

Sad at Watson's departure, I felt a burst of happiness too. His vocation, translator, so often lay buried behind the original author's more prominent name. Yet my life had been affected by his life's work, and I had been able to tell him so. The voice ringing in my ears these thirty years, dissolving time and space, was his.

ENCOUNTER WITH THE ARCH-TRANSLATOR

He reads Cold Mountain's poems slowly—
eyes swimming in the ocean of his father's gaze.
His warm tones soar like a Pacific breeze
over two continents, three thousand years,
one timeless practice—sitting still, making poems.
He is loud as one hand clapping, awake as a slap in the face,
radiant as his original face, a bug escaped from a bowl,
tears wet as a river longing for its home in the sea.

CHAPTER FOUR

PASSAGE TO MORE
THAN KYOTO

From the bullet train to Kyoto we watched Tokyo's suburban factories recede into groves of bamboo, islands of pine, hillsides speckled with dark tea bushes. A familiar snowcapped cone appeared in the distance, iconic Mount Fuji, inspiration for Japanese artists for millennia. Settling in, I pulled from my backpack Watson's translation of poems by the Japanese Zen hermit monk Ryōkan (1758–1831), a fellow follower of Cold Mountain.

I read that Ryōkan began training for a life as a village headman, the first son expected to follow his father's path. But he turned instead to a mountain hermitage to enter a life of meditation and poetry; no one knows why. I had an idea. An only son, like Ryōkan, I too was groomed from birth to follow the father's path, in my case a family business, a staple in Green Bay, nearly seventy-five years old when I was born in 1944.

Yet, as for Ryōkan, that golden suit of clothes held out for me, lovingly and generously offered, never seemed to fit. I recall from a young age a sense of discomfort at family praise that felt unearned, undeserved. So my drift away from my family's business expectations toward literature, although much slower than Ryōkan's, and quite painful all around, now felt to me a similar, inevitable step. Ryōkan became a Buddhist monk, then a hermit; I, like Cold Mountain, a husband and father. But in the end, we both found the path toward the mysterious energies of poetry.

Ryōkan took little with him to his mountain retreat, but he did bring his volume of his beloved *Kanzan*, Cold Mountain.

RYŌKAN NO. 35
Done with a long day's begging,
I head home, close the wicker door,
in the stove burn branches with the leaves still on them,
quietly reading Cold Mountain poems.
West wind blasts the night rain,
gust on gust drenching the thatch.
Now and then I stick out my legs, lie down—
what's there to think about, what's the worry?

I too read Cold Mountain poems after work, my fingertips reading and writing. I also worry—are my poems poems, or just another wayward enthusiasm? Ryōkan offered no comfort on this matter, mocking a "fine gentleman" who might look a lot like me.

RYŌKAN NO. 259
How admirable—the fine gentleman,
in spare moments so often trying his hand at poetry!
His old-style verse is modeled on Han and Wei works;

for modern style, he makes the T'ang his teacher;
with what elegance shapes his compositions,
adding touches that are striking and new.
But since he never writes of things in the heart,
however many he may turn out, what's the point?

My poems had better come from the heart, indeed, or "what's the point?" But how was one to know? Ryōkan offered little guidance here either, famously saying (in Watson's translation):

Who says my poems are poems?
My poems are not poems at all!
Only when you understand that my poems are not poems
can we begin to talk about poems.

Ryōkan's original name was Eizō Yamamoto, but he lived long enough to take two new names: Ryōkan, "Goodly Tolerance," and Taigu, "Great Fool." I was born halfway there. Lenfestey, old Norman French from the Island of Guernsey, means "one who is festive," from the same Latin root as "festival." I happily claim Feste, the fool in Shakespeare's *Twelfth Night*, as my spiritual ancestor, who said "Foolery, sir, doth walk about the orb like the sun; it shineth everywhere." But would I ever find my other true name?

RYŌKAN WROTE NO POEMS!
Ryōkan wrote his poems like Han-shan.
Who says I cannot do the same?

He asks only that the reader understand
that his "poems are not poems."
After forty years of practice,
I'm beginning to understand.
Now if I can only locate my heart. Is it inside
my head, my chest, my spine, or my pen?

CHAPTER FIVE

KYOTO KOAN

Kyoto's train station is an architectural amazement—part open-air Roman amphitheater, part megamall, part public square, part edgy warehouse district, part mountain waterfall. I know of no building like it, a modern wonder in a city famously ancient, its dozens of temples spared by Allied bombers during World War II as the repository of Japanese Zen.

We caught a taxi to our hotel on Gojo Street in a modern section of town, then found lunch in a soba noodle shop in an old storefront. Over steaming bowls of fresh buckwheat noodles in ambrosial broth, I examined a guidebook to the temples of the region, some massive World Heritage sites, others small and out of the way. Where to begin? In my left-handed way I thumbed from the back of the book, where I learned that the smallest temple, Shisen-dō, was decorated with paintings of thirty-six ancient Chinese poets. The temple was originally built as a hermitage by samurai Ishikawa Jozan in 1641, to spend his retirement seclusion as a poet. The portraits honored his literary ancestors. That would be tomorrow's beginning step.

The remainder of the afternoon we strolled gardens near the Imperial Palace and discovered Nishiki Shrine, where we happened upon a haiku festival. The entrance corridor of magenta bush clovers bloomed with white blossoms of paper haiku.

I tried my haiku hand.

At Nishiki Shrine,
clover flutters with haiku.
Mike looks. I listen.

✦

The bronze bell tolls one,
then another, slowly six.
Morning? Or evening?

✦

Mosquitos visit.
Crickets waken in the trees.
Sunset has arrived.

✦

Ravens call, caw caw.
Multicolored finches sing.
Go on, laugh at me!

After dark, we stumbled hungrily through a low, hobbit-style door into a wacky, akimbo restaurant near the Imperial Palace. In a room as dim as a cave, we sat next to a Japanese couple fluent in English and who loved poetry. We drank saki and recited poems back and forth all night, from haiku to Han-shan, tears of delight rolling down our cheeks. Only when we paid our bill did I register the name of the restaurant: *Ryōkan!*

Early the next morning we bought daily bus passes,

routes clearly described in pamphlets in a dozen languages, and were soon on our way to Shisen-dō, Mike rolling video-tape along the way.

The bus kneeled to drop us off, Shisen-dō a short uphill walk from the quiet street. Through a rustic wooden gate, we entered a low wooden hall where we bought tickets and replaced our street shoes with sandals before entering the temple grounds. I examined the portraits of Chinese poets scowling down above the moon hall. I did not recognize Cold Mountain, but these poets had called us to heaven.

A hush rose and fell over the garden, down from over-hanging maple and pine boughs, up from waves of raked white gravel and a gurgling rivulet muffled by a hedge. We sat on tatami mats on a platform open to this serene cosmos, mugs of whisked green tea appearing mysteriously at our elbows. A trickle from the stream fed the intermittent clack of a bamboo water clapper on the hillside. Designed to frighten deer from gardens, the clapper added the spice of sharp sound to the generous feast of murmuring brook, rustling maples, soughing pines, and whispering tourists unwinding their entire lives.

Navigating the Intelligent Bus System in Kyoto

We step from the bus at the Zen garden of Shisen-dō,
where paintings of Chinese poets hover above the
   moon hall.
Lighter with our shoes off, we float raked gravel waves
   like paper boats.

All morning we sit with tea frothed from a woman's
   deep sleeve.
Clack, clack, goes the water clapper, frightening no one.
Sigh, sigh, go the pine boughs listening overhead.
I do not know what practice put it right that we arrive here.
I do know the intelligent bus system will transport only
   our bodies home.

That afternoon we strolled Kyoto's medieval cobbled lanes, busy with tourists, and the vast plaza of a massive Buddhist World Heritage site, where Mike shot volumes of tape. In a small side garden, people hung origami birds of haiku from the trees. In a park we watched a man kite his haiku skyward. But it is our quiet morning at Shisen-dō, stillness radiant with sound, that lingers with me still.

That night, our last in Kyoto, we sought out the same soba noodle shop where we'd begun, where fresh buckwheat dough hung like leather straps from wooden dowels before it was cut into strips on wooden blocks, then placed into broths that fed the body and more. Transported out of my mind by morning peace and evening ambrosia, I managed to forget my backpack under our table in the restaurant, my travel documents trapped inside. I woke with a start in the middle of the night, realizing what I had done. Early the next morning, train departure looming, I ran to the restaurant and pounded my palm on the dark window glass. *What is the sound of one hand pounding?* A puzzled prep cook emerged from the basement stairs. He wordlessly lifted my pack into the air with a knowing smile.

We made the train, the gods again on our side, with

fifteen minutes to spare, only to board the wrong one. A kind conductor straightened us out, and we dropped at the next station to catch the right train eighteen minutes later. Although two days in Kyoto was a ludicrously short visit, I was relieved to return to the path toward Cold Mountain before I lost not only my head but my way as well!

CHAPTER SIX

RENDEZVOUS AT NARITA

One bullet train shuddered as another bullet passed until we arrived at Tokyo's Narita Station. We found Margaret and Ed waiting for us in the flight departure lounge. We greeted each other like old friends, thrilled to be embarking together into the literary heart of the Middle Kingdom. I marveled again at the magic that had brought us together, and ran over how it happened.

In 1998, with our last child nearly out of the house, I abandoned my sinecure on the *Star Tribune* editorial board to pursue the writer's path. After publishing a few small books, curating a poetry reading series, and founding a poetry festival, in 2005 I earned a residency at the Anderson Center for Interdisciplinary Arts in nearby Red Wing, Minnesota, a month of unencumbered writing time heretofore unknown in my adult life. I worked with Scott King, master of the press-in-residence, Red Dragonfly Press, to set twenty-two of my Han-shan-style poems in lead type, a meditative process that slowed my body and mind.

SETTING LEAD TYPE

Every piece is heavy, every movement slow.
Care of this kind one is not accustomed to.

That letter, is it worth the trouble? That sound,
is it really a bird fluttering, or a door closing?
When every sacred choice is made,
the lines are bound with a simple string,
tied with a common knot.
Every step that comes after—the paper, the ink,
the bookstore browser—reveals only the lightness.

I had brought with me a large carton of books on Chinese poetry and literature, treasures accumulated over several decades. When not setting type, I settled into my monk-like writer's cell at the Anderson Center to write and read. The first book I opened was *The Collected Songs of Cold Mountain*, translated by Red Pine, a bilingual edition published in 2000 but new to me. Stretched across the title page was a *photograph* of Cold Mountain's cave!

I couldn't believe it. Veiled in mist and mythology since the T'ang, a cave most scholars thought didn't exist suddenly had a physical presence. Could Red Pine, a.k.a. Bill Porter of Port Townsend, Washington, take me to the cave he had photographed? I wrote to the publisher but received no reply.

That winter I told the story of "seeking the cave" to Allan Kornblum, founder of Coffee House Press in Minneapolis, a friend with whom I regularly shared soup, sandwiches, and literary and family sagas. I mentioned the photograph I'd seen. Allan said the publisher used to work for him. A few days later I found Allan's voice on my office answering machine: "Don't say I never did you a favor. Here's Bill Porter's phone number."

I immediately punched in the number. A male voice answered. "Will you take me to Cold Mountain's cave?" I said. "Funny you should ask," Bill Porter responded. "I just brought a group of friends to China, to visit Buddhist shrines. You can be the second."

Right then we worked out the broad outline of the trip, a monthlong literary pilgrimage that would include visits to other poets' shrines along the way, ending at Cold Mountain cave. Only one hitch remained. To make costs affordable, Bill would hire a van for five passengers plus the driver. I needed to find three more pilgrims.

Mike eagerly climbed on board. He was a member of my raucous group of poetry lovers who met monthly for breakfast, when we routinely violated the well-known coffee shop admonition—"Please, for the benefit of yourself and those around you, no poetry!" Mike had a poet's ear as well as eye—most of his films were about poets and writers. Although unfamiliar with Cold Mountain, he was eager to document the madness.

But how would I find two more people with the time, resources, and spirit to undertake this strange pilgrimage? I had no idea.

That January my neighborhood bookstore, Birchbark Books, founded by novelist Louise Erdrich, hosted the first event for my handmade book, *Han-Shan Is the Cure for Warts*, published by Red Dragonfly Press. The room was packed, as much a tribute to Louise, who generously introduced me, and to my years of community activities, as to my poetry, known to only a few. Before I launched into my reading, I told the story of my discovery of the way to Cold Mountain, if only two more pilgrims would join me. After the reading, Margaret and Ed stood first in line at the book-signing table. "We want to go to China with you," they said.

I heard in the word "want" the kind of hunger I felt for this journey as well. They were not "interested," or "wondering," or "curious," or "debating" with spouses or co-workers. They offered an immediate "yes" to the wandering heart of this strange pilgrim journey. I offered an immediate "yes" in return.

Since then I had learned their story. Before moving to our Minneapolis neighborhood a decade ago, they had lived in Tokyo for three years, where Ed ran a high-tech company. They had visited business hotels in China but longed to experience the heartbeat of the country outside its shiny commercial islands, and they both revered books. Margaret, a feisty Canadian who had earned a master's degree in library science before entering business, served on many boards in the literary community. When Ed's outside businesses allowed, he did the same. And the timing was right, their two sons out of the house, one a practicing Buddhist.

Seasoned travelers, as Mike and I were not, they arrived at Narita with international cell phones and iPods stuffed with literature and music. Mike had his camera and a satchel of tape. I had my books, pens, and two empty notebooks.

In the departure lounge I glanced at an abandoned English-language newspaper, the last I would see for three weeks. The headline burned with the news that California grasslands were on fire, climate change coming home to roost.

Bashō wrote in 1692:

Summer grasses:
all that remains of great soldiers'
imperial dreams

He was echoing his literary ancestor Du Fu eight centuries earlier:

The whole country devastated
only mountains and rivers remain.
In springtime, at the ruined castle,
the grass is always green.

As a journalist who covered climate science for two decades, I could draw little comfort from that lineage of human folly, as glaciers melted, rivers ran dry, summer grasses burned.

The airline called our Beijing flight, and Ed and Margaret, Mike and Jim disappeared two by two into the ark of our own private Chinas one last time before touching down on the real China ahead.

NIGHT FLIGHT TO BEIJING

I tap my passport pocket,
fingertips thumping outside, heart inside.
Shaking all over, the Airbus lifts off.
Next to me, my friend sighs and sleeps,
resting sharp eyes for bright colors ahead.
Other friends relax, iPods chattering and singing.
In my lap, the old poems of China and Japan.
I scrawl my crude versions because my pen won't stop.

CHAPTER SEVEN

BEIJING: THE BIGGEST BELL
IN THE WORLD

Welcome to Beijing," smiled Bill Porter outside the airport gate, one hand impishly waving at the gray translucent haze behind him. He was wearing a blue bandana tied around his neck under an abundant beard, a T-shirt, beltless pants, a stuffed monk's bag hanging over his shoulder.

I had met Bill in person once before, in Port Townsend the prior June when I visited my daughters and grandchildren in nearby Seattle. I found him full of boundless energy with the irrepressible humor of a Han-shan. His blue eyes twinkled with delight. We worked out the details of our itinerary over green tea at his house high on a sand hill overlooking the Strait of Juan de Fuca. When finished, he took my arm and toured me around the wonders of Port Townsend, an old lumbering town experiencing an artistic renaissance.

His business card read "Translator." In addition to *The Collected Songs of Cold Mountain*—the book that brought us together—he had translated volumes by monks such as Empty Bowl and Stonehouse, plus pivotal Buddhist texts, all evidencing tremendous scholarship augmented by a life of Zen practice and unrivaled travel experience in China. After studying mediation in New York while studying Chinese at Columbia, he moved to Taiwan, where he remained from 1972 to 1991, living in two Zen monasteries until 1976. In 1991 he moved to Hong Kong, hired by a Hong Kong radio station to travel the mysterious mainland. Over two years he sent back more than a thousand two-minute audio stories—covering everything from traveling China's Wild West in a bus populated with drug smugglers to scaling the mountain aeries of forgotten hermits—before he returned to the United States in 1994 with his Taiwanese wife to raise his family. There could be no more knowledgeable guide to the literary and Buddhist landscape through the fun-house mirror of modern China.

Bill introduced the four of us to sweet-faced Mr. Chen, our driver for the first leg of our journey, a 1,100-mile trek to the ancient T'ang capital of Chang'an (Xi'an today), where Cold Mountain, like most literate Chinese, once battled the bureaucracy for a government job.

We loaded into Mr. Chen's new Toyota van for the short trip to the heart of today's capital city of nearly sixteen million people.

The oppressive grayness tasted of dust and smoke and pollution in some ghoulish brew, but the scramble of traffic—in Mr. Chen's calm hands—seemed not dissimilar from that of any urban megalopolis of the late twentieth century. Once-fabled bicycle traffic was crowded onto shoulders by the burgeoning car and truck traffic of the economic miracle. Ironic, I thought, as we Americans busily stripe our streets to add bike lanes.

I had read that the government cruelly swept away old city neighborhoods to build the forest of towers disappearing into the soup around us. But Bill somehow managed to find us rooms in a bed and breakfast down one of the remaining residential alleys, called *hutong*. After asking local directions once or twice, Mr. Chen guided our van, nearly scraping both sides, into a rabbit warren remnant of China's pedestrian past. A red door in a dusty terra-cotta wall opened into a quiet, modest courtyard, the residence of a once-famous opera singer. We registered, then collapsed into our beds for the night.

DAWN IN A BEIJING ALLEY

Only one cricket song for twenty million sleeping
    people?
How many hours since the last mosquito whine?
Already workers tap shiny new tiles,
hammer curbstones, spade in fresh shrubs.
Bicycle chains moan, trucks rattle and bang.
If only the air weren't crazy with soot and dust.
Wait, is that birdsong I hear? And a sweeping broom?
Only a neighbor brushing his teeth, washing his shirt.

After breakfast the next morning, Bill acclimated us to China time with a tour of Beijing's tourist splendors, beginning at Tiananmen Square, "The Gate of Heavenly Peace." We emerged from our taxi, immediately mobbed by eager vendors selling Little Red Books, dragon bells, and watches with Mao's hand waving and waving. I reflexively refused them all, not yet having a handle on the conversion of dollars to the "People's currency," renminbi (one to eight, it turned out). On one side of the vast public plaza, a long line of black-haired visitors in gray Mao jackets queued to pay respects at Mao's tomb, shuffling slowly forward like defeated soldiers. In the center of the plaza a massive, colorful "Olympic Clock" counted down the days to the 2008 Summer Olympics. Next to it a second garish construct, like a float in a Rose Bowl parade, celebrated the opening of the new "friendship" train to Tibet. I was happy we were taking neither trip. Bill pointed to a section of the square, cordoned off with yellow police tape, overseen by vigilant police. "That's where pro-democracy demonstrators were massacred in 1989," Bill said. Its emptiness stood out like a cry.

We visited the inner chambers of the Forbidden City, seat of imperial power since the fifteenth century, the entire complex rumored to contain 9,999 rooms. The last emperor, a boy, lived here only ninety-five years ago. Like Versailles, his house goes on and on, that old idea that leaders look only to mirrors for advice. Once a sage king asked a monk to take the emperor's job. He ran to the stream to wash out his ears! One emperor back in the T'ang, for love of a woman, laid down that big hat. Her garroted corpse lingered on the side of the road on which he attempted to flee, his capital in flames.

At the Big Bell Temple Museum, I paid extra—one hundred renminbi, eight dollars—to swing the mighty clapper at the thirty-four-ton mother of all bronze bells to send vibrations of cast Buddhist sutras radiating for miles.

I badly misjudged the arc of the clapper, a large log with a cushioned striker suspended from ceiling ropes, and barely dinged the ten-foot bell, to much tittering from the attendants and my group.

GONG-HO AT THE BIG BELL MUSEUM
When striking the mother of all bells, hit it hard!
The cast-bronze gong sends sutras vibrating fifty miles!
Even emperors could write a decent poem about this.
For a hundred renminbi a ticket, eight dollars US, swing!
All the mosquitoes in Beijing are waiting to tremble!

As we left the crowded city center, I was struck with an unaccountable paranoia that I had lost my backpack containing my journal, pens, and books, though it hung snug over my shoulder.

SEVEN REGRETS, FOUR BURDENS,
THREE ANXIETIES
Seven regrets:
failing to buy for my family five Mao watches,
one Little Red Book, one dragon bell
from the armless man at the Gate of Heavenly Peace.
Four burdens:
left-handed, dyslexic, forgetful, slow.
Three anxieties:
no pen, no paper, no books.

After lunch, we drove to the suburban Minghui Teahouse, a former Buddhist temple, where we spent the afternoon served by young women dressed in elegant long robes in a courtyard shaded by cypress trees.

Tea Ceremony at Da Jue Temple

Sweet wrists from black sleeves twist the aroma cup.
By the fourth infusion, we grow giddy with peace.
All around us, the baggage of Buddha.
Temple walls enfold groves of greenery.
Streams mumble prayers down rocky slopes.
Serving girls hide all delights but one under long
    monks' robes.
Cypress trees hush this place beneath their twisted capes.
For three hours my friends and I forget the teeming world.

CHAPTER EIGHT

IN XANADU DID
GENGHIS KHAN

For our final day in Beijing, we decided to skip the tourist-trodden Great Wall in favor of an extra hour's drive north to visit a thirteenth-century Silk Road postal station newly opened to tourists. Bill was curious to see Jimingyi, Cock Crow Station, constructed by Genghis Khan. I eagerly agreed. Long ago I had fallen under the spell of Coleridge's "Kubla Khan," memorizing its hallucinatory music. I knew the real Kublai Khan was Genghis's grandson, who built the "pleasure-dome" palace that so astonished Marco Polo on his visit in the thirteenth century and fueled Coleridge's laudanum dream in the nineteenth. I recited Coleridge's opening lines to convince my friends of the wisdom of Bill's choice.

> In Xanadu did Kubla Khan
> A stately pleasure-dome decree:
> Where Alph, the sacred river, ran
> Through caverns measureless to man
>   Down to a sunless sea.
> So twice five miles of fertile ground

With walls and towers were girdled round:
And there were gardens bright with sinuous rills,
Where blossomed many an incense-bearing tree;
And here were forests ancient as the hills,
Enfolding sunny spots of greenery.

Our "pleasure-dome," Mr. Chen's sparkling new Toyota van, pulled out of the *hutong* early the next morning for the two-hour trip to the Jimingyi Mountains. We stopped near a subway station to pick up two guests I had invited to join us for the day. Beijing University professor Jiang Feng was a colleague of my friend Al Lathrop Jr., the rare-book archivist at the University of Minnesota with whom I had worked to preserve the papers of the poet Robert Bly. Al described Feng to me as a World War II historian with whom he was working on a book about the Chinese front.

Imagine my surprise, then, when Feng and his companion, Ms. Chen, jumped into the van and he pressed into my hands a gift book of his translations of American poems! The text was in Chinese characters of course, but the table of contents, also in English, listed twenty-two American poets—from Whitman, Dickinson, and Stephen Crane to Plath and James Wright, my familiars! He smiled. "Al said you are poet, so I chose this book for you." I was speechless.

Feng looked much younger than his seventy-seven years, strong and vigorous, bald head glistening, eyes lively. Ms. Chen looked younger still, solid black hair cropped short, twinkling eyes, a sharp wit. As we drove into a freeway tunnel under the Great Wall winding above us like a writhing dragon, I asked Feng to tell us his story.

He fell in love with the English language as a student, publishing his first translations in college, and suffered immensely for his passion. He was denounced and imprisoned during the chaos of the movement against "rightists" in the late fifties. Then, as professor of English in the midsixties at the onset of Mao's Great Proletarian Cultural Revolution, he was banished with other intellectuals to the far mountains for a decade of hard peasant labor, losing all contact with his wife and two daughters. "You could visit your family four times a year, that was the 'policy.' But in the mountains there were no buses!" He dismissed with the back of his hand any earlier hardships, including years spent in Mao's army, which he considered an important duty. In fact, his career as a translator began as a "diversion" while he was working as an editor in the army. But the Cultural Revolution, he said, was "a nightmare." His eyes blazed. "A nightmare."

After the arrest of the Gang of Four in 1976, Feng established himself as editor of a literary journal near Beijing. In response to his bewildered nation's suddenly insatiable hunger for information about the West, particularly the United States, he located a dusty library copy of *American Modern Poetry*, edited by Louis Untermeyer, and translated the poems into the volume I held in my hand.

Since then, he had translated all the lyrics of Shelley, who symbolized for him the indomitable independent spirit. In fact, he had just returned from his own poetry pilgrimage to Shelley's grave in the Protestant Cemetery in Rome. And he had been the first to translate Emily Dickinson, in 1981, which caused a sensation, giving Dickinson her Chinese name, Aimili Dijinsen, in Pinyin. "Now poets in China try to write as Emily did," he crowed.

I asked Ms. Chen, a professor of petroleum geology, how she fared during the Cultural Revolution. She answered with a knowing smile, "Everybody went mad at that time. But even crazy politicians knew they needed energy."

The Jimingyi plateau was dry and yellow, like fall in Southern California, but the freeway was lined with fast-growing poplar trees, some plantings nearly thick as forests, an effort to catch the omnipresent dust in a nation scrubbing itself for Olympic visitors. There were millions, perhaps billions of these shiny-leaved poplar trees, a reforestation project on a scale only the centralized Chinese government could pull off.

Arriving at Jimingyi Station in late morning, we wandered the walls of the great Khan's crumbled empire, and the narrow streets of the rural village inside. At lunch at a tiny restaurant where we pulled together the only two tables, we toasted new friendships with beer, "*Gan bei*" ("Dry the cup"). Ms. Chen apologized for all the poor people around, and for the dryness. She was from a wet country, Wuhan, capital of Hubei Province, near a lake.

As we strolled the village streets after lunch, Feng and I talked like the oldest of friends. On a side street grown suddenly quiet after the passing racket of a two-stroke tractor, he stopped and leaned against the wall. He recited by heart two poems by Emily Dickinson, "Wild Nights - Wild Nights!" and "The Soul selects her own Society." Tears rolled down his cheeks, and he did not try to stop them.

As we drove quietly back to Beijing at sunset, passing again under the dormant signal fires of the Great Wall, my thoughts wandered over this latest unaccountable good fortune since setting out my intention to visit Cold Mountain. The man sitting next to me had been brutalized for the "crime" of translating poems. Yet I saw through the clear windows of his tears that the intimate intensity of those same poems had sustained him through hellish surroundings. "The soul selects her own society" indeed. From this "ample nation" of more than a billion souls, my soul had selected this one for me to meet.

TEAR IN HIS EYES

for Jiang Feng

Professor from a time when professors
were sent to fields to frighten birds,
he holds the tune of poems in his heart.
His callused hands set poems free
to feed prisoners time and worlds away.
Because of his tears, a billion people sing new songs.
And Chinese poets strive to write as Emily did,
words free to select their own society.

Mr. Chen pulled to a stop at a Beijing subway station and we bade good-bye to our new friends Professor Feng and Ms. Chen. Feng walked a few paces, then turned and shouted back to me, his eyes flashing, "You are my friend for life!" I felt the same, and vowed to bring him to America someday to feel under his boot soles the soil that nurtured the poetry he loved. As they disappeared down the subway stairs, I whispered to myself the final passage of Coleridge's Chinese dream:

> Weave a circle round him thrice,
> And close your eyes with holy dread,
> For he on honey-dew hath fed,
> And drunk the milk of Paradise.

CHAPTER NINE

JIA DAO AND THE RIDDLE OF SOUND AND SENSE

The next morning, guided by irrepressible Bill and in the capable driving hands of Mr. Chen (thank God, we were to learn soon enough), we set out to drive 1,100 miles across China's Yellow River basin and central agricultural plain toward the ancient western capital of Xi'an, stopping at important literary and spiritual markers along the way. In American terms, this was akin to meandering the Great Plains from Minneapolis to Denver by way of Kansas City, Wichita, Norman, and Amarillo, braking along the way for historical markers.

Bill sat in the front seat next to Chen, itinerary and maps in his hands, blue bandana secured around his neck, head cradled with a neck pillow "liberated" from his plane's business class. The rest of us spread out in the back, each with our own tools at the ready: Ed his 35 mm still camera, Mike his video cam, Margaret a fresh book cracked open, me a notebook and pen.

Our first stop, only a few dozen kilometers from Beijing, was the memorial shrine to the T'ang Dynasty poet Jia Dao (779–843), whose poems are recited today by schoolchildren throughout China, as Cold Mountain's rough colloquial poems decidedly are not.

We were the only visitors. A female guide brightened when she saw us, and eagerly chatted us through the garden courtyard surrounding Jia Dao's grave, a six-foot-high mound of earth covered in grass like uncombed hair. A freshly painted mural in the shrine hall illustrated the tale, famous in Chinese literature, of Jia Dao's fortunate accident. After abandoning a monk's life for that of a poor poet in the world, he was traveling on his donkey one day absorbed in the bottomless problem of choosing the exact word/sound to fit a poem. Should it be "knock" or "push" in the line "In moonlight, a monk (knocks? pushes?) the gate"? As he rode, lost in thought, his donkey stumbled into the sedan chair of a high official, spilling him to the ground. Fortunately, that official was Han Yu, Confucian poet and teacher as well as important public administrator. So instead of cutting off Jia Dao's head for such careless effrontery, Yu recognized that such absorption in sound and sense was the mark of a true poet. Han Yu offered Jia Dao friendship, not a death sentence.

That's as good a story of the poet's life as I know. After stupefying labor to match right sound with right sense to make the bones of a poem sing, the lucky poet gets a grant, the unlucky one the death sentence of oblivion. Either way, the labor goes on.

I thought of my own mysterious absorption. Sometime early in my schooling I read, with millions of others, Robert Frost's poem, "Out, Out—." What struck me was not the heartbreaking outcome of the narrative, shocking and sad as it was, but the layers of sound and sense Frost crafted into his opening lines: "The buzz saw snarled and rattled in the yard / . . . And the saw snarled and rattled, snarled and rattled, / As it ran light, or had to bear a load."

SEEKING THE CAVE

I remembered the vibration of "snarled and rattled," the short, speedier vowels in "as it ran light," the slow-throated long vowels in "had to bear a load," imitating the saw's sound and action. Reading the poem, I registered for the first time the internal music of poetic language rather than its more obvious and familiar meter and rhyme, how language could be fashioned to work in several dimensions at once. I have been in thrall to that music ever since. Now an old man with a white beard, I still seek to capture the apt syllable, for the past thirty years with the rhythm of ancient Chinese poems ringing in my ears.

In his essay "Six Disciplines That Intensify Poetry," Robert Bly describes the lure of "ancient friendships between sounds." All people recognize them, Bly writes, "but it is another thing to take part in their arriving—to put out a call for sound friendships, to decide to encourage certain ones. Then we are awake by one more degree. To be awake as a writer is to take part in sound friendships and welcome them."

Here in distant China, in a small township near Beijing, I was awakened to one more poet seeking "ancient friendships between sounds." Chinese culture has absorbed Jia Dao's lesson well. According to his best translator, Mike O'Connor, "The compound 'push-knock' (*t'ui-ch'iao*) became thereafter the traditional term to describe not only Chia Tao's [Jia Dao's] assiduousness of craft, but any poet's exacting labor to find the *mot juste* or make careful stylistic distinctions."

I was on the right trail.

Morning Travel

Rising early
to begin the journey;
not a sound
from the chickens next door.

Beneath the lamp,
I part from the innkeeper;
on the road, my skinny horse
moves through the dark.

Slipping on stones
newly frosted,
threading through woods,
we scare up birds roosting.

After a bell sounds
far in the mountains,
the colors of daybreak
gradually form.

(by Jia Dao, translated by Mike O'Connor)

BOOK II

FROM BUDDHIST TEMPLES
TO SOARING CRANES

CHAPTER TEN

BUDDHISTS FOR THE NIGHT

Buddhist Bill booked us two nights at Bailin Temple a half day's drive from central Beijing, where a beaming, shaved-headed monk greeted us at the iron gate. He walked us swiftly through a maze of internal courtyards and complicated corridors under winged cornices to surprisingly modern guest quarters—airy double rooms with tatami mats over bed frames, showers with intermittent, sulfur-smelling hot water, electric lights, and a thermos of hot water left at the door twice a day. In other words, far better than expected. Founded in 1347, the temple's fortunes rose and fell with the various dynasties, the latest depredation an invasion by the Red Guards in 1966, the year I graduated from college. Today Buddhism is rehabilitated and so too this ancient temple, gleaming once more.

We returned to the town's dusty main street for dinner. Bill rejected the first restaurant when he found it also housed a brothel, not uncommon here, he said. He located a family restaurant where we gamely chewed gristly meat inside dry, crumbling wheat biscuits. As we tumbled back into the van eager for our monastery mats, Bill revealed with a grin that the restaurant specialized in donkey meat. "It was the best place open, so I thought we might give it a chew."

I woke at first light to a strange, repeated rattling, both in my stomach and outside the window. A monk slapped a split bamboo clapper on courtyard stones, the monastery's call to breakfast.

BAILIN TEMPLE, DAWN
Bad tatami mat sleep, burping last night's donkey gristle.
Many dreams, all lost before dawn.
Cold/warm/cold/warm shower, sulfur-smelling water.
Dressed in shirt washed by hand, jeans, everyday sandals,
I wrote in my journal how I missed my wife in Beijing.
Then prepared green tea. Now I am happy
to meet the smiling faces of a hundred monks alone.

Gathered outside, the five of us watched a procession of bronze-robed monks and black-robed nuns glide quietly from the massive meditation hall where they had been chanting sutras since four. We fell in behind them, following along into the dining hall, silently taking seats on benches at long wooden tables facing a raised table on which sat the abbot. Each place was set with wooden chopsticks and a single stainless metal bowl into which apprentice monks ladled a gruel of thin oatmeal, followed by rice, a few stir-fried vegetables with tree-ear mushrooms, and a steamed roll. Bill had hastily briefed us on dining hall etiquette. Monks sit at the inner tables, pilgrims at outer tables. No one lifts a chopstick until the abbot has raised his bowl, and all stop when he stops. No speaking. I soon learned as well that one who leaves food in a bowl receives a sharp scowl from the server. I decided to turn down future rolls, a spongy sop flavorless as paste.

After breakfast, Abbot Minghai, an old friend of Bill's, sent word he would meet us for afternoon tea. We spent the morning with other pilgrims exploring the extensive grounds of gardens and buildings ancient and modern under a dusty sky. We were surprised when a woman in a Western-style suit spoke to us in American English. A principal researcher for the Taiwanese tea industry, she had earned her doctorate at UC Davis. A Buddhist, she made an annual pilgrimage to Bailin, which, she said, had an ancient connection to tea. "The first temple to tell pilgrims to drink tea," she said. She showed us her research into the antioxidant effects of certain teas. Her Buddhism, however, was a quiet, personal affair, nothing to say. Bill agreed. "The more you understand Zen, the more you realize how little you need to understand it. This is why intellectuals have such a hard time. They can't get that it is so radically simple."

How I admired that calm. So many of the T'ang Chinese poets were touched by Buddhism, inspired by its inward journey, including Cold Mountain. But though I was finally on Cold Mountain's path, I could not shake my Protestant sense that if the world needed fixing, I needed to try to fix it.

That afternoon a monk ushered five American pilgrims into Abbot Minghai's modern, spacious office. The walls and bookshelves were covered with photographs of former abbots and construction cranes raising the new chanting hall of ten thousand Buddhas, the largest in China. We sat on low cushions facing Minghai, who was seated cross-legged behind a low tea table elaborately fashioned from a tree stump. A vibrantly handsome man about forty with a wide, captivating smile, he spoke good English, the residue of a degree in English and philosophy from Beijing University.

Attendant monks delivered high mountain tea and a thermos of high mountain water, considered as important an ingredient as the tea itself. The abbot refilled our small cups through seven infusions as we talked, mostly in English, the entire afternoon.

Bill and Minghai recounted how they first met at Bailin in 1989, during Bill's first search for traditional Buddhist hermits, chronicled in his 1993 book *Road to Heaven*. Bill had attained "a state of fearlessness," Minghai said, and we nodded in agreement, already well on our way to figuring that out.

We asked Minghai how he had decided to become a monk. He laughed. When he found himself sitting in the lotus position on his university professor's desk, he realized university life was not his path!

Margaret proudly told him that one of her college-aged sons was a devoted student of Buddhism. Ed asked clear questions. Bill sat straight-backed, attentive to every utterance. Mike was so serene the abbot noticed him first. I dared recite a poem I had scratched out since breakfast that morning.

BREAKFAST WITH ONE HUNDRED MONKS
AT BAILIN TEMPLE

One hundred monks raise their bowls of gruel,
like waves gently slapping an anchored hull.
Apprentice monks serve them, ladles knocking
stainless steel pails like the clang of stays.
Robes rustle like wind in bronze sails.
The sweet-faced abbot steers his ship
from the bridge using only delicate chopsticks.
He drives very slowly, all eyes resting upon him.

Minghai broke into a great laugh at the final line, and soon talked openly about the strains of the abbot's job. Like most religious leaders these days, he was a tireless fund-raiser. He was proud of his latest accomplishment, the enormous new chanting hall of ten thousand Buddhas next door. But if not reappointed for another five-year term, a decision to be made by his fellow monks, he aspired to live in a quiet meditation hut in the mountains. He offered to build a hut for me as well! Though a hut described exactly the size of life I longed for, I turned him down. I had not yet traveled far enough on the road to Cold Mountain.

I asked one final question: "The tea is so fragrant. Is it the high mountain water or the high mountain tea?" Minghai responded with a grin and a whoosh of his robe as he raised his cup to his lips. "Here is my answer to that!"

AFTERNOON TEA WITH THE ABBOT
High mountain water, high mountain tea—
the perfume lasts a dozen conversations.
The abbot flaps his bronze wings
toward mountain solitude.
From the cushion where I sit,
light outlines his shaved head
and runs in gold down his warm shoulders.

Before dawn the next morning, Mike and I eavesdropped outside the main meditation hall, mesmerized by the waves of chanted sutras flowing from the open door in golden light. Abbot Minghai once said to Bill, "You could say that the activities of a Zen monastery don't depend on words, only sounds. As the meditation hall resonates, so does the rest of the monastery." Perhaps the rest of the world resonates too.

After the monks departed, we wandered inside. The red temple walls were lined with golden images of Buddha, each about a foot tall, literally ten thousand of them covering three walls. In ritual Buddhism, repetition of Buddha's image is good, more repetition is better, ten thousand an ultimate number. In the center of the hall, a larger-than-life statue of the Buddha quietly raised an expressive finger. Outside, doves chanted their mourning mantra as the sun limped over the horizon through a dark curtain of dust and pollution.

THE TEMPLE OF TEN THOUSAND BUDDHAS
Two walls of small golden Buddhas, five thousand each,
scatter their reflections all around.
At the heart, a seated Buddha big as a boulder
signals the inner universe with one slim finger.
A solitary monk swishes back and forth his bristle broom.
Outside, the sun, like a pale moon, cannot part the
    curtain of dust.
In the cypress grove beyond the walls, doves call in
    strange voices.
Beyond them, the chatter of ten thousand tongues of
    drying wheat.

After breakfast the next morning, Abbot Minghai bade us farewell at the monastery gate with a generous wave and another radiant smile. Then he pivoted to take a dusty call on his chiming cell phone.

CHAPTER ELEVEN

BREAKFAST WITH CONFUCIUS

October 3, 2006. Qufu.

Entering the walled city of Qufu, Confucius' hometown, we had missed by only a couple of days his 2,557th birthday on September 28, but the celebration was still going strong. There is no solid evidence for this birth date in 551 BCE, but, as Bill said, "There's no evidence it's *not* true. That's the camp I'm in. Prove it's *not* true."

We threaded the gauntlet of street vendors and souvenir shops that by 8:15 a.m. were already thronged with Chinese tourists ready to visit Confucius' shrine. After purchasing tickets, we entered the shade of a serene "welcome forest" of gnarled juniper trees said to be half a millennium old, then followed a path sheltered by two rows of three-hundred-year-old black locusts to the shrine's formal entrance.

Several large halls spread their winged cornices across the park-like setting, at the end of which lay Confucius' grave mound, the size of a large hill, befitting his stature as China's master moral philosopher. In China, the greater your status, the higher your grave mound, and Confucius articulated a system of human relationships that has guided China's search for social and political harmony for 2,500 years. His Chinese name, *Kong tze*, means Master Kong, *Confucius* the Latinate translation familiar to Western ears ever since it was given to him by Jesuit missionaries in the sixteenth century.

I ate a delicious yam roasted over charcoal—crusty, hot, and sweet—purchased from a street vendor, and meditated on the world Confucius made.

Visiting the shrine of Master Kong felt like visiting Mount Vernon, the Vatican, and the Library of Congress all rolled into one. Scholar as well as teacher, Master Kong legendarily compiled all five of China's required great books, including the *Shih Ching: The Book of Songs*, arguably the world's first poetry anthology, the title of which became the word for lyric poetry itself, *shih*. I was eager to pay my respects. I recited to the others a teaching of Master Kong I have long cherished:

> The Master said, Little ones. Why is it that none of you study the *Songs*? For the *Songs* will help you incite people's emotions, to observe their feelings, to keep company, to express your grievances. They may be used at home in the service of one's father; abroad in the service of one's prince. Moreover, they will widen your acquaintance with the names of birds, beasts, plants and trees.

That translation is by Arthur Waley (1889–1966), the Burton Watson of the first half of the twentieth century. Like

Watson a brilliant scholar of Asian languages, he abandoned his sinecure at the British Museum for the translator's path. In 1917, Ezra Pound published Waley's first translation from the Chinese in the *Little Review.*

Pound's own translations—not really translations but gifted "versions" worked up from the journals of Asian scholar Ernest Fenollosa—radically transformed the form and sound of English-language poetry in the first half of the twentieth century, the way Kenneth Rexroth's, Robert Bly's, James Wright's, Gary Snyder's, and W. S. Merwin's Chinese-inflected poetry did for many of us in the second. According to Eliot Weinberger, Pound's 1915 collection of Chinese versions, *Cathay*, "was the first great book in English of the new, plain-speaking, laconic, image-driven free verse."

In his book *East Window: The Asian Translations*, Merwin tells the story of the effect on him of his discovery of that form and sound.

> By the time I was sixteen or so I had found Arthur Waley's Chinese translations, and then Pound, and was captivated by them both. Their relations to the forms and the life of the originals I will never be able to assess. But from the originals, by means and with aspirations that were, in certain respects, quite new, they made something new in English, they revealed a whole new range of possibility for poetry in English. Poetry in our language has never been the same since, and all of us are indebted to Waley and Pound whether we recognize it and acknowledge it or not.

Robert Bly acknowledged the same debt. In a 1998 interview with the *Great River Review,* Bly and William Duffy, cofounders of the influential literary magazine *The Fifties,* revealed the "principal aim" of their magazine:

> Our aim was to bring spontaneity to American poetry similar to the spontaneity in classical Chinese poetry which was just then being translated on a larger scale. In that sense we wanted to dissolve some of the English forms—not necessarily because we hated them, but because they were more skeletal than vital. Those Chinese poems represent a different kind of sophistication than the English model. There were things that we yearned for that we found in this poetry. For one, Chinese poetry always dealt with nature. Secondly, there was a real playfulness. Third, maybe was that transcendental thing.

Like any good poet, Confucius believed the "rectification of names"—getting the names right—was essential to bringing the world into proper harmony. "Collect from deep thoughts / the proper names for things," Lu Chi advised in the third century, quoting Confucius.

Bill told us Master Kong's birthday was now a national holiday, Teachers' Day, which, it struck me, would be an excellent addition to the US holiday calendar as well. As a journalist covering education and the environment during the nineties, I was horrified by the chorus of mostly Republican politicians and politically conservative bloviators vilifying America's teachers as money-grubbing slackers, a slander badly undermining respect for the profession. A national Teachers' Day might help rebuild it.

To "rectify" the name of "teacher" was a battle my Confucian temperament would once have eagerly engaged— the same way I'd worked for decades to restore the voice of the earth to human ears. But today I was on the path of a different teacher. Cold Mountain was schooled on Confucius, like every literate Chinese, yet ended his days scribbling alone in a quiet cave. His poems voice a search for private, not public, order after the bonds of society have crumbled to dust.

The birthday of Cold Mountain will never cause a nation's celebration. A common man of common speech and common struggle, he would have laughed at such a vanity, not devised a system to embrace and control it, as did Master Kong. Cold Mountain meditated on luck and longing, and disappeared in joyful dance, like Zorba embracing "the full catastrophe" of the individual, not the communal, life.

Although I now walked Cold Mountain's path, I would forever admire China's exemplary teacher Master Kong. As even Abbot Minghai recognized, someone has to answer the dusty cell phone.

Leaving Confucius' call behind, we stopped for dumplings and noodle soup at an outdoor restaurant near Qufu. We admired the view of a range of hazy mountains considered sacred in the Daoist tradition. A delightfully mistranslated marker identified the tallest peak as "Mountain of the Nine Imnotls." On the spot, we adopted "The Five Imnotls" as the moniker for our pilgrim band on our decidedly mortal wanderings.

CHAPTER TWELVE

SPEEDWAYS, CORN ROADS,
AND APPLE LANES

Much of our driving took advantage of China's brand-new freeway system, like America's in scale and scope only in better shape, with information signs in both Mandarin and English. If only the Chinese could drive!

In the cities traffic proved to be an unchoreographed ballet of bicycles, scooters, three-wheelers, vans, cars, and trucks all weaving together, including random left, right, and U-turns, propelled by a sixth sense of trust, what Buddhists call karma, Americans call luck. On freeways, the same rules applied. No matter what, keep driving. We somehow survived Mr. Chen's unnerving pace through miles of blinding fog, twice coming upon epic freeway pileups. Thanks to Mr. Chen's karma, our luck was to live another day.

In search of the remote gravesite of the philosopher Zhuangzi (369–286 BCE), the most famous interpreter of Daoism, we spent a long day in the countryside navigating a newly paved two-lane highway. Local farmers had colonized half the warm concrete as a solar grain dryer, so Mr. Chen slalomed slowly for tens of miles around checkerboard squares of drying corn, millet, and peanuts while dodging roadside chickens, goats, children, elders, dogs, bicycles, motorbikes holding three or four people, three-wheelers hauling carts bulging with cornstalks and babies, tractors out of gas (we helped push one out of the road), gas stations out of gas, and nearly washed-out bridges with muddy approaches. We stopped to ask directions several times from roadside walkers. "Zhuangzi?" They all knew who he was. A few knew where he was.

The corn surprised me. I had expected wheat and millet this far north in China, not midwestern American corn. "Pig food," Bill explained. Farmhouse roofs were piled high with golden mounds of kernels while bundles of dusty stalks lay stacked against household walls for winter fuel.

Stubble fire smoke added to the autumn haze. Farmers with hoes turned powdery fields one more time toward winter wheat. White-scarved mourners paused in one field to plant a fellow farmer under a mound of earth, soil tilled his entire life, long or short, like a thousand generations before him.

I admired the meticulously groomed fields tended by women in tight black pants and colorful jackets and by ageless, smooth-faced men. Many had returned from the cities to help their families harvest. Some slept on cots by the side of the road.

We arrived at Zhuangzi's shrine in fading afternoon light, though hard to tell, with daylight dusky, the sun only a circle of crimson. Bill was surprised at the changes since his last visit. A wall and entrance gate surrounded the shrine, previously open to the surrounding fields. Inside, we admired

Zhuangzi's large grave mound, fifteen feet high, befitting a stature eclipsed only by Laozi and Master Kong. Several fresh stone steles commemorated recent visits by Daoist pilgrims from Japan, France, and Thailand.

Only a few found their winding way to Zhuangzi's shrine, so local farmers had planted the grounds with melons and spread the paving stones with drying corn. A toothless elderly woman squatted on the paving tiles, picking up stray kernels, while local children mobbed us with curiosity.

Zhuangzi told the story of the man who sought out Laozi to find a solution for his problems. Laozi asked him, though he had arrived alone, "Why did you come with all this crowd of people?" Laozi saw the invisible baggage of old attachments we all carry with us. Our visible as well as invisible baggage as American visitors attracted much attention and generosity wherever we went in the countryside.

Zhuangzi left us an impish paradox I love:

> The fish trap exists because of the fish; once you've gotten the fish, you can forget the trap. The rabbit snare exists because of the rabbit; once you've gotten the rabbit you can forget the snare. Words exist because of the meaning; once you've gotten the meaning, you can forget the words. Where can I find a man who has forgotten words so I can have a word with him?

According to Burton Watson, Zhuangzi employed the device of koan-like non sequiturs "that jolts the mind into awareness of a truth outside the pale of ordinary logic." No wonder lyric poetry and Zen practice, called *Ch'an* here, were invented in China. The people had already been struck by Zhuangzi's wordless lightning!

Driving to our hotel late that starless night, we were stuck for miles behind a chuffing two-stroke tractor with no headlights or taillights, hauling long dark wooden poles swaying dangerously behind like a dragon's tail. Ghostly outlines of pedestrians haunted the sides of the road. Bill was relieved when we finally reached our hotel in the railroad city of Shang'qiu. Had we not, "Any of those farmers would have insisted on giving us their food and beds," he said, a burden we did not want to impose on already heavily burdened people.

A day later, on the way to a second remote shrine, we bumped down a long two-track through an extensive apple orchard, branches brushing both sides of the van. Ravenous, we stopped to pick a few apples, the ordinary ones, not those on the trees already individually wrapped in plastic bags against pests and the omnipresent dust and pollution. Hearing the van stop, farmers and their families materialized from under nearby trees. With huge smiles, they thrust apple after apple into our hands.

Near Jinan, sacred Mount Tai emerged from the haze. Although we had no time for a climb this trip, we knew all must climb it someday, where all spirits go.

CLIMBING TAI SHAN
Over Dai Miao Temple, sacred Tai Shan
looms through autumn haze.
Confucius climbed it.

Mao Zedong climbed it.
Bill Porter climbed it.
Someday, all must climb it,
this place where spirits go.
What a long climb!
What a lovely view!

We climbed instead nearby Stone Gate Mountain, the only foreigners on the path, our first rendezvous with two of the T'ang's greatest poets, Li Bai and Du Fu. We hiked up a dry streambed, then up several steep stone stairways. Up a final flight, straight up, we suddenly entered the compelling presence of a monk patiently guarding the door to his temple. His fiercely gentle eyes under a burnished head indicated he was not surprised to see us. As I placed a ten-renminbi note in his wooden box, he expressionlessly dinged a bronze bell with a wooden clapper.

Accompanied by two sprightly, laughing young women who served as volunteer "guides," we hiked farther up the trail along a sheer mountain wall to a lonely, wind-sculpted rock outcrop. A pagoda marked the spot where, it is said, Du Fu and Li Bai once met back in the T'ang.

Ahh, Li Bai, you swashbuckling Byronic exotic in love with poetry and wine! Ahh, Du Fu, you heartbroken poet-official bearing the weight of the fallen world on your slim shoulders, idolizing Li Bai's ethereal gifts. What a thrill to feel your sacred presences.

Our "guides" returned to their parents, and we sat quietly under the open-air pagoda in a swirling wind. I pulled from my backpack Bill's *Poems of the Masters: China's Classic Anthology of T'ang and Sung Dynasty Verse*, originally compiled at the end of the Song Dynasty (960–1279). During the T'ang and Song, poetry pervaded every sector of literate society: administrative court, chanting temple, teeming marketplace, and lonely outposts from which officials lamented their enforced separation from family and friends. "Every occasion required a poem," Bill wrote in his preface. On the occasion of our first encounter with Li Bai and Du Fu, I read out loud Bill's translation of Li Bai's famous quatrain:

SITTING ALONE ON CHINGTING MOUNTAIN
Flocks of birds disappear in the distance
lone clouds wander away
who never tires of my company
only Chingting Mountain

Then Du Fu's lonely *shih*:

RECORDING MY THOUGHTS WHILE
TRAVELING AT NIGHT
A shore of thin reeds in light wind
a tall boat alone at night
stars hang over the barren land
the moon rises out of the Yangtze
how could writing ever lead to fame
I quit my post due to illness and age
drifting along what am I like
a solitary gull between Heaven and Earth

Picking our way slowly down Stone Gate Mountain at sunset, the Five Imnotls fell into quiet meditation. As daylight disappeared, we reached the van where faithful Mr. Chen smiled up at us, apparently as relieved at our return as we were at our freeway survival.

Back on the road, all of us quiet, I felt as if we were beginning to lay claim to new names. On earlier rides, Mike and I had dreamed up new names for our pilgrim band. Bill of course was Red Pine, the name under which he had already established his reputation as a translator of poetry and Buddhist texts. He told us he took the name from a Taiwan billboard advertising Black Pine Cola. "Red seemed the more Chinese color," he laughed. An apt choice, I thought. Bill's hardy North American namesake, the red or Norway pine, grows straight and true in rough conditions and, like Bill, is self-pruning, minimizing clutter.

As a child of the Great Lakes, I had always felt an exceptional affection for white pine, our tallest, most elegant native tree, with solitary black arms and fingers of long, surprisingly silken needles. I planted a family of white pine with my grandfather the summer he died. I remember every detail and I was not yet four years old. The wind sings six decades later through those dark branches leaning over the eastern shore of Green Bay, a shrine I try to visit every year.

"Jack Pine" seemed the perfect name for Mike. A scrappy nonprofit filmmaker, he earned his living cobbling together film after film from a random assortment of small grants and smaller donations, plus gigs teaching filmmaking to kids around the North Country, including on Indian reservations.

His documentaries explored poets, peacenik nuns, a trickster Anishinabe storyteller, reclusive artists, and the antiwar senator and poet Eugene McCarthy. His ear was as attuned to poetic sound as his eye to poetic sight. So Jack Pine he became, for that scrappy resident of northern granite islands and sand plains where most other trees simply give up.

Back in the van, new names continued to flow. Ed, a West Point graduate with a strong, straight spine and sweet, soft heart, became Lodgepole Pine. Fearless Margaret was of course Foxtail Pine, the strongest and most enduring of all. "So many names fill the mind-sky," said Bill.

CHAPTER THIRTEEN

ORDINARY AND
EXTRAORDINARY GRAVES

D riving the freeway through thick fog toward Dengfeng, we came upon the smoking remains of another epic freeway pileup—trucks crumpled, cars sliced and burned, a bus with a grim body image imprinted on its shattered windshield glass. Fortunately we were too late to see the bodies themselves, or to be among them.

The fog cleared into a vista of broad farm fields groomed and tilled, not an errant leaf under a power line or grove of trees. Some fields held earthen mounds three or so feet high, six feet in diameter, old ones crowned with wild vegetation, new ones darkened with fresh earth—bodies returned to the land that nourished them.

ON SEEING A DAOIST PILGRIM BY THE
SIDE OF THE ROAD

I cannot forget you, cinder in my passing eye.

How filthy you were.

How you swayed back and forth in a verse's recitation.

How the shredded soles of your sandals told tales of
distant journeys.

How your staff, a peeled stick, said you walked alone.
Rocking back and forth on the seat of my tourist van,
I wonder how I became I, you became you,
both to be buried under a mound of earth in a dusty field.

We were in search of the family grave of the greatest poet of the Song Dynasty, Su Dongpo (1037–1101). His birth name was Su Shi, but he is remembered by his literary name, Dongpo, "eastern slope," which he took from his small farm home in Hangzhou. Like his father and brother, he became famous not only as a poet but as a calligrapher, essayist, and public servant, although his satiric poems brought him much harassment and exile.

Su Dongpo shines especially bright for me through one of those satiric poems I first heard recited by poet Bill Holm at the Minneapolis Public Library nearly two decades ago.

ON THE BIRTH OF HIS SON
Families, when a child is born
Want it to be intelligent.
I, through intelligence,
Having wrecked my whole life,
Only hope the baby will prove
Ignorant and stupid.
Then he will crown a tranquil life
By becoming a Cabinet Minister.

I laughed out loud when Bill recited it by heart, and asked him to send me a copy. A few weeks later a photocopy arrived, taken from an edition of Arthur Waley translations published

SEEKING THE CAVE

by the Book of the Month Club in 1940. Bill carried that
poem in his huge Icelander chest for years, and now I carry
it inside me, reciting it to particularly knowing approbation
during the incompetence of the George W. Bush Dynasty.

Once again we were the only tourists at a shrine, this one
to Su Dongpo, his father, and brother, "the Three Sus." It
was a serene setting, with racks of incense burning pungently
before three large grave mounds shaded by a brace of ancient
cypress trees. A handful of locals lingered under the trees.
A farmer, proud of his physical fitness at eighty-two, told us
he and his wife came here regularly to relax in the shade and
read the sutras. We relaxed in the shade and read Bill's translations of Su Dongpo from *Poems of the Masters*.

SPRING NIGHT
   A spring night hour is worth a ton of gold
   the pure scent of flowers the moon's pale light
   music from the terrace finer than silk
   swinging in the courtyard far into the night

FLOWER SHADOWS
   Layer upon layer on the alabaster terrace
   I tell the boy to sweep them up in vain
   just as the sun takes them all away
   the full moon brings them back again

We had neither sun nor moon nor shadows during
these murky days, but my heart was full, my mind slowly
breaking away from the business of the busy world.

Our final stop that day was a cave made famous by the

founder of Zen (*Ch'an*) Buddhism in China, the Indian monk Bodhidharma, who lived in the fifth or sixth century. Like Bill a blue-eyed Buddhist barbarian, in this case most likely from southern India, Bodhidharma is said to have stared wordlessly at the cave's wall for nine years to purify his mind. Bill, a Zen practitioner since his college days in New York in the seventies, never failed to pay homage when in the neighborhood.

The cave lies high in the Song Mountains behind Shaolin Temple, world famous as the founding home of the martial arts. Bodhidharma is kung fu's unlikely patron saint. The village streets near Shaolin bristled with four-story academies housing thousands of students from dozens of countries, a sort of martial arts Disneyland. Cadres of boys in bright uniforms thronged sidewalks, marching to their lessons. Mr. Chen parked near the town square, and we walked past a central performance stage where students flashed swords and lances in remarkable feats of disciplined derring-do to a deep disco beat. A crowd watched mesmerized, lured in by a tout with a bullhorn. I was as entranced as the others, watching in slack-jawed amazement, but soon enough Bill pulled us away from the carnival-like chaos toward its opposite, Bodhidharma's quiet mind.

"Flowers is loveable. We ask you not to injury," a tourist sign requested along the footpath past the temple grounds. We "loveably" lifted our feet toward the nearby mountain slowly revealing itself through late-afternoon haze. At its base, 1,500 stone stairs climbed out of sight above us. At 4:00 p.m., only a few fellow pilgrims were making the climb.

A Norwegian couple counted each step—the platform where we spoke was number 978, the cave still a black dot high above us. Two Chinese couples, the men in coats and ties, the women in fashionable blouses and tight black pants over high heels, apparently didn't notice the heat and humidity, while the Norwegians and Imnotls perspired freely. As we climbed, mountain crags appeared across the valley under the first blue sky we'd seen since Beijing.

The steps terminated at a narrow ledge twenty feet long, a dark opening at one end hardly tall as a man. We were pleased to find the wooden door to the cave still open this late in the day, a black-clad nun sitting before it at a low, candlelit altar.

Bill hastily demonstrated the proper ritual to use before entering:

- Light incense.
- Hold stick against forehead.
- Bow.
- Place incense in holder before seated nun.
- Bow lower, place forehead on cushion.
- Rise and put palms together.
- Repeat two times.
- Then pray with hands together.
- The nun will chime the bronze bowl at each prayer, and each time money is placed in the box.

We prayed. We donated. She chimed. We entered.

Small as a hobbit hole and black with soot, the cave was apparently perfect for what Bodhidharma had in mind, which was to leave his busy mind right here. We sat, paying silent homage to the founder of Chinese Zen, who said: "Seeing your nature is zen. . . . Not thinking about anything is zen. . . . Everything you do is zen."

Then we stepped meditatively down the 1,500 stone stairs toward the path of "loveable" wildflowers below, then past the ten thousand tourist distractions of Shaolin Temple. Back at the van, Bill, undistracted, said, "Let's eat!"

Some say Bodhidharma's body is buried in one of the dozens of other caves on Song Mountain, nobody knows which one. We do know his clear mind now travels the entire world, wondering when the rest of us will follow.

CHAPTER FOURTEEN

DU FU'S SORROW

October 6, 2006

After a wordless, eye-popping drive the next morning toward the city of Gongxian southwest of Luoyang, we reached the family compound of Du Fu (712–770), whom Kenneth Rexroth called "the greatest non-epic, nondramatic poet who has survived in any language."

ROADSIDE ATTRACTIONS ON THE ROAD TO
DU FU'S GRAVE
Shoulders heaped with holy boulders.
Concrete quilted with golden corn.
Diesel generators like giant insects.
A hundred men shaping stone with mallets.
Ten thousand astounding sights will not keep
me from your shrine, Du Fu.
Not even the stone steles of Emperor Truth,
nor the man dead by the side of the road
beneath his load of shifted bricks.

This was only one of Du Fu's three burial shrines, the grave mound here most likely containing his robe and hat. The tomb said to hold his body is in Hunan Province, and Burton Watson describes a third site as now "a veritable national shrine to the poet's memory," Du Fu's "thatched hall" along Wash-Flower Stream near Chengdu, where he settled happily but all too briefly from 760 to 762.

I walked the lush grounds as slowly as possible, not wanting to leave. I especially admired the twelve-foot-tall statue of Du Fu. The sculptor rendered him rail thin inside a full-length robe, his stooped shoulders set against the sky.

Much of Du Fu's adult life was cursed by famine, flood, the death of a child, and the catastrophic social breakdown of the eight-year An Lushan Rebellion, which devastated the social structure and the countryside, killing or displacing possibly two-thirds of the tax roll population. Du Fu was arrested, exiled, and forced into much lonely travel, his body failing while still on the road in his fifty-eighth year. Only more than a century after his death did his greatness become clear, a fate that would surprise few poets and certainly not Du Fu.

To Pi Ssu Yao

We have talent. People call us
The leading poets of our day.
Too bad, our homes are humble,
Our recognition trivial.
Hungry, ill clothed, servants treat
Us with contempt. In the prime

Of life, our faces are wrinkled.
Who cares about either of us,
Or our troubles? We are our own
Audience. We appreciate
Each other's literary
Merits. Our poems will be handed
Down along with great dead poets'.
We can console each other.
At least we shall have descendants.

(translated by Kenneth Rexroth)

Days before, under the winged cap of an open pagoda as wind circled a darkening sky, I read aloud to my friends Du Fu's heartrending ballad, "Song of the War-Carts," translated by David Hinton, the greatest antiwar poem I know of in any language.

SONG OF THE WAR-CARTS

War-carts clatter and creak,
horses stomp and splutter—
each wearing quiver and bow, the war-bound men pass.
Mothers and fathers, wives and children—they all flock
alongside, farewell dust so thick Hsien-yang Bridge
disappears. They get everywhere in the way, crying

cries to break against heaven, tugging at war clothes.
On the roadside, when a passerby asks war-bound men,
war-bound men say simply: *Our lots are drawn often.*
Taken north at fifteen, we guard the Yellow River. Taken

west at forty, we man frontier camps. Village elders
tied our head-cloths then. And now we return, our
hair white, only to be sent out again to borderlands,

lands where blood swells like sea-water. And Emperor Wu's
imperial dreams of conquest roll on. Haven't you heard
that east of the mountains, in our Han

                                 homeland, ten hundred towns and
ten thousand villages are overrun by thorned weeds,
that even though strong wives keep hoeing and plowing,
you can't tell where crops are and aren't? It's worst for
mighty Ch'in warriors: the more bitter war they outlive,
the more they are herded about like chickens and dogs.
Though you are kind to ask, sir,
how could we complain? Imagine
this winter in Ch'in. Their men
still haven't returned, and those
clerks are out demanding taxes.

Taxes! How could they pay taxes?
Even a son's birth is tragic now.
People prefer a daughter's birth,
a daughter's birth might at least end in marriage nearby.
But a son's birth ends in an open grave who knows
where. You haven't seen how bones from ancient times
lie, bleached and unclaimed along the shores of
Sky-Blue Seas—how the weeping of old ghosts is
joined by new voices, the gray sky by twittering rain.

The laments of Du Fu's life felt distressingly familiar to me in post-9/11 America, along with the memory of a sweeter, saner time. Like the post–World War II America of my youth, the T'ang Dynasty opened with a long period of political stability and economic prosperity under a government that embraced progressive politics and the arts. Then it descended into years of internal rebellion that mirrored, in mood if not in intensity, the Kennedy, Johnson, Nixon, and Bush administrations' collapse into hubris, paranoia, and aimless marching armies. No one escaped the later T'ang turmoil, certainly not Du Fu. Sorrow settled deep into his bones like an incurable cancer.

SNOW STORM
Tumult, weeping, many new ghosts.
Heartbroken, aging, alone, I sing
To myself. Ragged mist settles
In the spreading dusk. Snow skurries
In the coiling wind. The wineglass
Is spilled. The bottle is empty.
The fire has gone out in the stove.
Everywhere men speak in whispers.
I brood on the uselessness of letters.

(translated by Kenneth Roxroth)

If the joy of my life began with books, marriage, and children, the sorrow of my life began with the war in Vietnam. Brought up solidly Confucian, to respect and follow fathers and leaders, my generation faced the forked road of war or rebellion, no win possible either way. An old poem of mine tells the tale.

At the Vietnam Memorial

His name ambushed me out of black granite, a college
  friend.
And with his death, a vow revealed carved on my heart
these thirty years: We who stayed must also pay.
They carried dead back to the chopper, we only carried
  water.
This is the way it is for us who did not go,
no matter how hard we fought to save those crouched in
  this black wall.
There is no release from this blood vow
'til our names too
are carved on polished stone.

My father and I fought for a decade over the Vietnam War, which I opposed and worked hard to end, while he, good Confucian, insisted that the president, even a despised Democrat, must be followed in time of war, the only right path. So I knew something of Du Fu's shattered family and, in post-9/11 America, the choking dust of fallen dreams.

Driving Across Wisconsin, September 11, 2001

Do the trees know what happened?
Is that why that one's crown
is rimmed with fire, that one's arm

droops a flagging yellow?
Sumac, thick as people
on a crowded street,
redden suddenly from the tips.

Ferns in dark hollows of the forest
reveal their veins.

Bouquets of asters, purple and white,
offer themselves from the side of the road
to all the wounded passing by.

Leaving Du Fu to his mourning, we turned again toward the open road. The atmosphere outside mirrored my dark mood with ground-hugging pollution we could taste, the sun only a pale memory. At lunch I asked Mr. Chen, who grew up in this region, if the air was this thick every harvest season. "No," he answered, "it is pollution (*wu ran*). I have never seen it this bad."

CHAPTER FIFTEEN

BAI JUYI'S "IDLE DRONING"

October 7, 2006, on the way from Luoyang to Lingbao

In Tokyo, I'd learned that the prolific Bai Juyi (772–846) was one of Burton Watson's favorite poets. So I was happy we were visiting his memorial shrine a short boat ride across the Yi River from the Buddhist carvings at Longmen Grottoes, a World Heritage site south of Luoyang. At Longmen, we strolled past a limestone cliff carved with thousands of images of the Buddha and his disciples, some an inch tall, others massive muscled guardians of a Buddha nearly sixty feet high, most dating from the late fifth century through the T'ang. When Mike, a diabetic, felt his energy run down and decided not to climb the stairs into the largest cave, I was so stunned by what I saw inside I returned and pulled him up by the hand.

We rode a motorboat shuttle across the river to the quiet eastern bank where monks once lived in caves. This was the poetic landscape and Buddhist sensibility Bai Juyi came to love after retiring from a "long and checkered career as a government official" in the capitals of Luoyang and Chang'an (Xi'an).

In the gift shop—a blackened monk's cave with intermit-tent electric light—I bought a Bai Juyi poem for Watson in fine calligraphy executed before us by a gentleman-scholar said to be Bai Juyi's descendant. That 1,200-year genealogy mind-boggled this visiting American, though it was hardly uncommon in China with its obsessive record keeping. At Bai Juyi's nearby grave, elderly Mr. Jung, a volunteer caretaker devoted to Bai Juyi's verse, recited by heart several poems at our request. Though I could understand no words, his dra-matic gestures and streaming eyes filled me with admiration, like watching a conductor moved by a great symphony.

IDLE DRONING

Since earnestly studying the Buddhist doctrine of
    emptiness,
I've learned to still all the common states of mind.
Only the devil of poetry I have yet to conquer—
let me come on a bit of scenery and I start my idle droning.
            (*by Bai Juyi, translated by Burton Watson*)

"A rapt appreciation of the ordinary," Watson wrote of Bai Juyi, who even in Buddhist retirement would revise his poems over and over again if even one of his servants could not understand it.

Returning across the Yi, our water taxi driver coughed constantly, evidence of the nasty respiratory problems com-mon to those breathing this hideous pollution. Environmental catastrophe was something Bai Juyi would have taken on in his feisty younger days in the capital. Later he spent whatever

money he had on public works. He built a dike to stop river
flooding and to provide drinking water. Like his poems, they
have lasted to this day.

MISSING MY WIFE AT LONGMEN GROTTOES
Climbing eighty stairs to the hall of carved stone
    Buddhas,
I wanted to hold your hand. Look, his house is as big
    as ours!
I wanted you to hear the old man with shining eyes
recite Bai Juyi's poems from beyond the grave,
one hand beating his chest like a heart, the other
floating like a boat departing a river of tears.
But I did not miss you back inside our crowded van,
another long, hot drive through grime and haze ahead.

CHAPTER SIXTEEN

WHAT THE OLD
MASTER WROTE

From the ancient capital of Luoyang to the ancient western capital of Xi'an, a loess plateau rises below the western mountains holding back the Mongolian high plateau. Millions of years of dust blown from the high desert settled here in giant drifts hundreds of feet deep. Fine as face powder, loess is the secret ingredient of early Chinese prosperity. It can be plowed with a wooden stick, requiring no metal implements. Chinese farmers have turned it over productively for ten thousand generations, life from dust.

We stopped on the way at Hangu Pass, the place where, it is said, Laozi set down the immortal *Dao De Jing*. We had to pay our respects.

A natural cut in the loess, the pass afforded an easy spot for the emperor to post guards to control barbarian traffic into the empire. It also proved an easy place to stop an old man riding his water buffalo slowly the other way, determined to leave behind the chaos and corruption of city life to seek the clarity of solitude. That is the story, anyway, and standing between two towering walls of yellow dust, I felt it to be true.

In 1972 I purchased a beautifully illustrated *Tao Te Ching* (*Dao De Ching*), translated by Gia-Fu Feng and Jane English, that still honors my bookshelf. Their *Dao* arrived in my life at the moment the honor of my civilization was crumbling to dust in Vietnam, and I read it with astonishment. The polar opposite of Confucius, Laozi insisted one find one's own path by consulting the mysterious flow of nature, not the predictable vagaries of men. "A journey of a thousand miles starts under one's feet," Laozi said.

> Therefore the sage goes about doing nothing, teaching
>   no-talking.
> The ten thousand things rise and fall without cease,
> Creating, yet not possessing,
> Working, yet not taking credit.
> Work is done, then forgotten.
> Therefore it lasts forever.

As we stood between the walls of compressed dust rising over our heads on both sides, I recalled that tear in the fabric of my generation, repeated again, and as mindlessly, by the war in Iraq. I imagined the guard, himself war torn and weary, now bored and lonely, stopping an old man's mysterious passage. Why west, why alone, why toward nothingness?

"Please, sir, sit down. Teach me what you know. I have a brush. I have ink. We have time. We will write it down together. The desert above us is boundless. The cities behind us war without end. Your bones can wait a few more days to disappear into dust."

It is said the guard may have recognized Laozi as a revered teacher, once keeper of the archives at Luoyang. Some say Laozi was 88 years old, others 160, others 996. Maybe he was 62. We know only that he lived long enough to have something eternal to say. Thus the world gained the *Dao De Ching*, five thousand words about what cannot be expressed in words.

> The Tao that can be told is not the eternal Tao.
> The name that can be named is not the eternal name.
> The nameless is the beginning of heaven and earth.
> The named is the mother of ten thousand things.

Nearby, visiting schoolchildren climbed a high battlement and shouted their delight to companions below. I kept my journal and pen in my backpack, silent and still. What could I possibly say?

CHAPTER SEVENTEEN

THE SOARING CRANES
OF XI'AN

We departed Lingbao early the next morning after an American-style breakfast at the insanely named Zingy Good Hotel, a Japanese-financed, twenty-three-story round glass tower, neat and spotless and empty, its panoramic windows overlooking a gloom of pollution, dust, and morning mist.

On the road from Beijing to Xi'an we often passed coal-fired power plants hurling clots of dense gray smoke, sometimes accompanied by cumulus clouds of steam boiling up from massive wasp-waisted cooling towers. I had heard there were many nuclear power plants in China, and of course the epic Three Gorges hydroelectric dam, and some dramatic new solar and wind installations, but all we ever saw were angry coal-fired dragons belching crude smoke, the kind that America tamed with the Clean Air Act more than thirty years ago. Thanks to electricity, life is easier for humans living on China's agricultural plain, but breathing is harder. Much harder. As for the natural life of the planet, everywhere heartbreak. A desperate old poem of mine once tried to grasp it.

Climate Change

Winter comes to the north, wary now, a wounded
    predator,
toppling weakened spruce, falling through thin ice.
We raise our torches and howl all the long nights
against the Emperor burning brush on southern ranches.
But he is warring again, blind in acrid smoke, deaf to
    keening.
Our voices hoarse, our tears pathetic, flow like raging
    melt water
where polar bears drown and giant sunfish befuddle in
    Arctic seas.

The sky cleared to blue just east of Xi'an as we neared
the famous archaeological site of the Underground Army.
Ever since its discovery was publicized in the late 1970s, I
had wondered why on earth an emperor would choose to *bury*
armed guards expected to protect him into eternity. Now I
learned why—because he could. The loess here is two hundred feet deep.

Qin Shi Huang (259–210 BCE), China's legendary
founding emperor, united the warring provinces in 221
BCE, creating essentially the China we know today. Qin's
(pronounced *Chin*) many astounding achievements include
standardizing roads, laws, weights, measures, and currency;
establishing the meritocracy; building the first Great Wall;
and unifying the Chinese script so that forever after China's
texts could be understood, if not pronounced.

On the dark side, he ordered the burning of most of China's

already ancient books, including the *Book of Songs*, the *Shih Jing*, and buried alive 460 scholars who were said to protect them, a feat of eradication of "old ideas" unparalleled until Mao's Great Proletarian Cultural Revolution surpassed him a hundredfold, as Mao himself exuberantly recounted.

To ensure the immortality of his city-sized mausoleum, Qin had entrances booby-trapped with automated cross-bows and buried alive the thousands of artisans and others who might disclose the treasures inside. The First Emperor succeeded handsomely in keeping his secret, for not until 1974 did farmers thirty kilometers outside Xi'an, digging a well, clunk into something that sounded oddly ceramic.

As it was already afternoon, we hurried past the quarter-mile gauntlet of tourist shops flanking the entrance toward a spectacular wing-like metal enclosure. Inside, we gazed down upon rank after rank of life-sized terra-cotta warriors emerging from powdery loess to march another day. I could almost hear their muttering voices, the creak of the war-carts, the twittering rain.

For tourists, this discovery is a great victory, and we were certainly awestruck at the sight. But I will forever prefer the compassionate poetry of *Song of the War-Carts* to an emperor's megalomaniacal dreams.

Each of the terra-cotta warriors is said to have an individual face, an extraordinary artistic achievement. But I saw not one eye wet with tears, either of laughter or sorrow.

CHAPTER EIGHTEEN

ROAD TO HEAVEN

Under clear skies for the first time in eleven days, Mr. Chen's dusty van glided at dusk through the sharp-edged city walls that encircled the ancient capital city of Xi'an, now a tourist mecca. We registered at the Big Bell Hotel near a winged bell tower looming over one end of the old city, an equally dramatic drum tower marking the other.

Bill apologized but said he needed to rush off to a nearby bookstore. His Chinese publisher, taking advantage of our itinerary, had set up a publication celebration of the translation into Chinese of Bill's classic 1993 book, *Road to Heaven: Encounters with Chinese Hermits.* Bill told us he dreaded such events but agreed to this one to honor his publisher's enthusiasm and the efforts of the translator, an old college friend of Abbot Minghai's. Although dusty and hungry, we said we were happy to follow our bright-eyed guide wherever he led, even into the heart of the Ka-ching.

So after a quick cleanup in our rooms, we hurried after Bill down ancient Xi'an's narrow, busy streets. We were surprised by gleaming, ultra-modern Wan Books and by the boisterous crowd of well over a hundred jammed inside, including several bronze-clad monks and black-clad nuns. The bookstore manager, clearly relieved at Bill's arrival, ushered us through the crowd to seats flanking a coffee table piled high with freshly printed books with a photo of our bushy-bearded guide on the back cover.

Road to Heaven chronicles Bill's adventures with photographer Steve Johnson in the "hermit heaven" of backcountry China in 1989 as they sought out monks and nuns still on the "path of solitude" after a century of war, revolution, and repression.

> Steve and I left the Sian [Xi'an] area and continued our odyssey across central China, climbing other mountains, talking to other hermits. Most of them were Buddhists, but many were Taoists; most were monks, but many were nuns; most were old, but many were young. They were all poor, but they had a way of smiling that made us feel we had met the happiest and wisest people in China.

Judging from the crowd's eager attentions, Bill's book must have felt like a family reunion with revered ancestors presumed dead since the Cultural Revolution, when Red Guards smashed shrines and compelled monks and nuns out of their mountain retreats into "productive" work in state farms and factories. Bill's disclosure that the hermetic tradition was still alive seemed as important to Chinese Buddhists as the discovery of the terra-cotta warriors was to the Chinese tourism bureau.

As we watched from the sidelines, Bill stood at the microphone and spoke in Mandarin for fifteen minutes about his road to heaven, then answered questions, the audience alternately laughing with him and assiduously taking notes on his comments. He sat down to a wave of applause, after which several monks and a starstruck student took over the microphone for extensive complimentary orations, blessedly cut short when the bookstore staff emerged with a huge birthday cake for Bill, sixty-three years old that day. The whole room sang "Happy Birthday" in the universal melody. Who knew that our impish, dogged leader was a birthday boy, not to mention a Buddhist rock star?

That night we wandered the public plaza where vendors sent battery-powered handmade tops sparkling with lights spinning and dancing over the ancient cobblestones. I bought four, a dollar each, for my four grandchildren. Cold Mountain, Bai Juyi, Du Fu, and so many others made youthful plans for sparkling lives inside these powerful walls of hewn stone. Only the poems remained, hymning the inner life enveloped in mists beyond the walls of power. As Bill wrote:

> Throughout Chinese history, there have always been people who preferred to spend their lives in the mountains, getting by on less, sleeping under thatch, wearing old clothes, working the higher slopes, not talking much, writing even less—maybe a few poems, a recipe or two. Out of touch with the times but not with the seasons, they cultivated roots of the spirit, trading flatland dust for mountain mist. Distant and insignificant, they were the most respected men and women in the world's oldest society.

CHAPTER NINETEEN

FIRST ADVENTURE
IN HERMIT HUNTING

The next morning, Bill led us on an expedition into the nearby Chungnan Mountains, where his own hermit-hunting journey had begun more than twenty-five years before. We planned to visit the Buddhist nun whose serene portrait graced the cover of *Road to Heaven*. We would not seek out the nearby Wang River hermitage of T'ang Dynasty poet Wang Wei, also nearby. Bill had assaulted that mountain redoubt in 1989 only to be arrested for his efforts; Wang Wei's reclusive paradise was now a nuclear weapons facility.

POEM BY WANG WEI
in my prime I loved the Way
a Chungnan cottage in old age
when I want I roam alone
wonders wasted all on me
hiking to the river's source
sitting watching clouds arise
sometimes with an old recluse
talking laughing free from time
(translated by Bill Porter)

Feeling "free from time"—mistakenly, it turned out—we stopped on the way out of town to pay our respects at Big Wild Goose Pagoda in Xi'an's southern suburbs. At seven stories the grandest pagoda of the T'ang, it enshrines the accomplishments of the extraordinary Buddhist pilgrim and translator Xuanzang (circa 602–664). A seventh-century Bill Porter, he famously traversed the Silk Road from Xi'an (Chang'an then) to India seeking Buddhist education, shrines, and texts. He returned seventeen years later with relics of the Buddha, a brace of statues, and, most importantly, 657 sutras. He devoted the rest of his life to their translation from Sanskrit, and some of them became the foundational texts of Chinese Buddhism. At the insistence of the emperor, he also wrote down his pilgrim story, inspiring the famous sixteenth-century fictional account *Journey to the West*, considered today one of the four Chinese classics. Arthur Waley's abridged translation made it famous in the English-speaking world as *Monkey*.

Margaret, Ed, and I climbed the pagoda's narrow stone stairs to the seventh story, from which we could see modern Xi'an swaddled in thick mist stretching to the mountains. From one south-facing window, Margaret counted thirty-one tower cranes piercing the haze, busily raising apartment blocks, factories, suburbs, and, as Mike and I were to learn soon enough, an entirely new university campus. In ancient China, the dancing, long-legged crane was sacred. In the Ka-ching Dynasty, it's the tower crane.

Back on the highway toward the mountains, Mr. Chen's driving karma was soon sorely tested. A massive red dump truck traveling in the opposite direction inexplicably lurched a U-turn right toward us. We watched wide-eyed and speech-less as it slid just past our rear bumper and broadsided a smaller truck right behind us, bulling it over onto its side with a mighty *ka-whump*. Locals arrived to deal with that driver's bad karma as we traveled on in grim silence.

After several map consultations to extricate us from the swiftly expanding suburbs, Mr. Chen finally navigated us onto the narrow road to the far mountains. We wound along a thin ribbon of hairpin turns cluttered with construction debris. Below us a reservoir filled behind a new hydroelectric dam. Margaret, otherwise a tiger of travel, was not at all pleased with her backseat view into that azure chasm, and lay down on the seat until the drive was over.

Bill was surprised when we arrived at our destination to find the pristine side valley he remembered filled with the chaos of freeway construction. A million stilts of bamboo strode across the mouth of the valley between two dark holes emerging from one mountain and two dark holes bored into the other, another freeway through the unstoppable Ka-ching.

Nevertheless, we donned our daypacks and soon enough the scaffolds and construction noise receded behind us as we hiked up a well-worn footpath along a rushing stream. As we passed a small village with front doors open to footbridges over the water, a few villagers emerged to look us over. One recognized Bill and they shared a word.

At a persimmon tree, Bill paused for a moment, then led us onto a red dirt trail winding steeply up the mountainside toward the hermit's aerie high above us. Resting on boulders along the way, we admired poems we found carved on trailside bamboo, the way Han-shan may have carved some of his poems 1,200 years ago.

After numerous switchbacks and much perspiration we reached the crest, only to find an abandoned farmer's hut, not the nun's hermitage Bill expected. Puzzled, he led us along a ridge trail toward a wisp of smoke rising in the distance. The farm family there was more than a bit surprised to see visitors, not to mention five Westerners. They said they knew nothing of our hermit nun. Bill realized that he must have taken the wrong turn at the persimmon tree, and that the nun's hut was on the other side of the valley, a distance now several hours' hike away. Remaining afternoon light would not permit that trip. "Well, we always bag our hermit," Bill said with a grin, "just not today."

WRONG TURN AT THE PERSIMMON TREE

High mountain breeze praises the hermit of our dreams.
High mountain stream tumbles her story past village
doors.
We climb and climb, wet with sweat, pleased with the
pleasant view.
Resting, we admire fresh poems carved on green bamboo.
Did hermit poets prepare this place for us,
turning point under the blue bowl of heaven?
Turn right at the persimmon tree, or you will never know.
Turn left at the persimmon tree, or you will never know.

Back down the steep foot trail and the gut-wrenching highway hairpin turns, we arrived on the outskirts of Xi'an just as the sun disappeared over the city. Bill made a cell phone call. "She's disappointed," he said. "She had prepared lunch for us." Hermits with cell phones?

HERMITS WITH CELL PHONES

Head shaved, think of the trouble and money saved!
No shampoo, no conditioner, no dye, no lice!
For a pillow, a shaped stone, for a mattress, reed mat.
Thatched roof keeps out rain, a few sticks and the tea
    fire crackles.
A flat piece of ground grows melons and beans.
Pilgrims, bring me tea, salt, a small jar of oil, your
    dreams.
When you visit, I'll serve you what you need.
Call my cell phone first, and I'll be ready!

CHAPTER TWENTY

AN EVENING WITH DR. HU

We soon learned even cab drivers get lost in booming Xi'an. I was scheduled to discuss poetry that evening with Dr. Hoover Hu's literature class at Northwest University, a connection made through Bill Holm, who taught there in 1988 and 1991 and lived to tell about it in his hilarious survival guide, *Coming Home Crazy: An Alphabet of China Essays.*

Late from our failed hermit hunt, Mike and I hastily jumped into a cab, Bill giving the driver the name of the university. He and the others would follow in the next cab. Our driver dropped us at a dimly lit campus entrance and pointed wordlessly down a concrete walkway. The security guard at the entrance shook his head, mystified by the building and room numbers we showed him. At the doorway of a dingy concrete building, we flagged down two passing students. A lucky hit, they were eager to practice their English. Looking at our papers, they recognized immediately that the cab driver had made a mistake, and sprang into action. They flagged down a second cab, piled in with us, and rode the half hour to what proved to be an entirely new campus. This one looked like a Skidmore, Owings and Merrill design from the

1960s, with well-lit broad concrete walkways between starkly modern horizontal buildings.

Dr. Hu rushed up to greet us at the curb, his relieved smile revealing the gleam of a gold tooth. His black, heavy-rimmed glasses and long, shiny hair parted in the middle gave him a Yeatsean flamboyance. A prominent translator, he had superb English. Seeing us in proper hands, our new friends sped away, refusing all offers of money or thanks for their time or cab fare.

Hoover guided us swiftly to his classroom. By now hours late, I imagined it would hold at most a handful of hostile, restive students. Instead, it was packed wall to wall with a hundred black-haired, dark-eyed students patiently waiting and wondering, with Dr. Hu, why a white-bearded, blue-eyed American would travel all the way to China to seek the cave of Cold Mountain.

Dr. Hu introduced me as the "poet from America I have been telling you about, who loves Cold Mountain." He offered me the podium and took a seat in the front row. The roundtable discussion I had imagined was apparently lost in translation, and I realized that, in our hasty departure, I had brought no books. I would have to proceed by heart.

I asked the students if they understood English and, see-ing a wave of black-haired nods, asked them to stand with me and recite my poem, "Wasted Hands," following my hand and arm movements. It is a poem of mine I sometimes use to startle audiences out of the lassitude common at too many poetry readings back home. With obvious delight and much laughter, the students recited the lines one by one after me, mimicking my gestures.

WASTED HANDS

These hands are wasted.
Yours too.
No grace without gesture,
yet palms fold only in toward prayer.

We turn ours out.
And in that simple rotation
catch a power carved in ochre
on black rock ten thousand years ago.

We touch our thumb and index at the tips,
and turn our palms toward you,
the way smiling India statues do.

Now raise our hands in heaven's praise!
Then sweep them wide as wings
to build a nest of palms and brushing thumbs
beneath the Buddha's heavy-lidded gaze.

Since I was the mysterious American "who loved Cold Mountain," I recited several of Watson's Han-shan translations by heart. After each, Hoover read the original in Mandarin from a bilingual edition. Had I known then that Han-shan's poems are not so beautiful in Mandarin, I might have been embarrassed, but instead I felt nothing but joy.

COLD MOUNTAIN NO. 39

The birds and their chatter overwhelm me with feeling:
At times like this I lie down in my straw hut.
Cherries shine with crimson fire;
Willows trail slender boughs.
The morning sun pops from the jaws of blue peaks;
Bright clouds are washed in the green pond.
Who ever thought I would leave the dusty world
and come bounding up the southern slope of Cold Mountain?

I told them I too never thought that I would leave my world of Confucian responsibilities to bound up the southern slope of my own Cold Mountain, the mysterious cave of poetry, to mutter and write as I pleased. But after a busy life as parent, teacher, businessman, and journalist, I could no longer resist Cold Mountain's call.

I recited other poems to illustrate features of English-language poetry I loved. I had memorized "The Lake Isle of Innisfree" decades ago from an old recording of Yeats's stubbornly musical voice. As I recited, I noticed Hoover in the front row moving his lips along with my words, tears in his eyes. He later told me it was his favorite poem.

THE LAKE ISLE OF INNISFREE

I will arise and go now, and go to Innisfree,
And a small cabin build there, of clay and wattles made:
Nine bean-rows will I have there, a hive for the honey-bee,
And live alone in the bee-loud glade.

And I shall have some peace there, for peace comes
    dropping slow,
Dropping from the veils of the morning to where the
    cricket sings;
There midnight's all a glimmer, and noon a purple glow,
And evening full of the linnet's wings.

I will arise and go now, for always night and day
I hear lake water lapping with low sounds by the shore;
While I stand on the roadway, or on the pavements grey,
I hear it in the deep heart's core.

I had the students sound out the last line's long "eeee,"
long "aahhhrrr," endlessly long "oohrrr," like "roar," echoing
the poem's "deep heart's core."

I pointed out the poem was written when Yeats was a
young man living alone in London—"young like you," I
said—and describes his prescient dream of the reclusive life,
one many eventually seek, one Cold Mountain somehow
found.

Then I recited the "sprung rhythm" of Hopkins' "Inversnaid,"
pure poetic music gracing an urgent plea. Listen as if to a symphony, I said, and conducted with my hands as I recited.

INVERSNAID
This darksome burn, horseback brown,
His rollrock highroad roaring down,
In coop and in comb the fleece of his foam
Flutes and low to the lake falls home.

A windpuff-bonnet of fawn-froth
Turns and twindles over the broth
Of a pool so pitchblack, fell-frowning.
It rounds and rounds Despair to drowning.

Degged with dew, dappled with dew
Are the groins of the braes that the brook treads through,
Wiry heathpacks, flitches of fern,
And the beadbonny ash that sits over the burn.

What would the world be, once bereft
Of wet and of wildness? Let them be left,
O let them be left, wildness and wet;
Long live the weeds and the wilderness yet.

I ended with Robert Bly's little-known poem of powerful images, "Waking Up," his singular American take on the fundamental Buddhist concept of awakening.

Waking Up

When he wakes a man is like the earth
Rolling over, as it rolls at dawn, turning
Jagged mountains gradually and grasslands
Up to the fierce light of space.

Something in me remembered all night
To breathe on as I slept.
The breath protected me, as the atmosphere
Around the earth protects the earth.

When I was a small boy I like to think
I thought once it would be best to die.
That would make everything better
For others, and knives flew around the house.

At dawn I resemble a soldier who wakes after a battle,
His friends all dead, and himself still alive.
What do I do? I walk through the ditch grass,
Skirting the towns, asking in barns for fresh milk.

"How does one 'wake up' in your world?" I asked.

As the class ended, Mike, who had hastily set up his video and audio equipment, asked the students to recite a poem back to us. We listened as one hundred voices intoned in unison Jia Dao's famous quatrain "Looking for a Recluse but Failing to Find Him."

Under the pines I questioned the boy.
"My master's off gathering herbs.
All I know is he's here on the mountain—
clouds are so deep, I don't know where . . . "

The poem resonated in Mandarin chorus, like a rhythmic chant. Little of that music survives in any English translation I could find after the fact, even this one by Burton Watson. As Hoover dismissed the class, the students offered a round of applause for what Hoover called "a real poet." I felt a flush of embarrassment at a designation that had baffled me my entire life.

Hoover insisted on entertaining Mike and me at a late dinner with a few handpicked graduate students. In the cafeteria, a shiny glass and stainless steel affair comparable to that of any American college or university, Hoover ordered huge platters of skewered chicken, multiple stir-fries, and a half dozen beers. We swirled chopsticks while he smoked incessantly and we talked poetry, literature, and life. A pretty graduate student with hair dyed auburn in the artist's fashion aspired to study the novel at Princeton with Toni Morrison. A skinny poet hoped to continue his writing, but was sensibly studying business. I asked him to read one of his poems, and we listened intently around the table to his Mandarin music.

"Are you Buddhist?" he asked me after his reading, tapping the bracelet on my wrist made from prayer beads. I had forgotten I was wearing it, a gift from Abbot Minghai. "No," I answered, "I'm not Buddhist. Nor a hermit. I'm just seeking what they sought—the cave of solitude after a busy life."

"What is in the cave?" the novelist asked. "What is it you seek there?" "I don't know," I answered. "That's why I'm here."

Hoover accompanied us to our hotel and refused to allow us to pay the cab fare, so I vowed I would send him a stack of books. After saying our grateful good-byes, Mike and I realized that we'd never had time to miss Bill, Ed, and Margaret, last seen looking for a taxi to follow us. At breakfast the next morning we learned their taxi couldn't find the campus either. They gave up and returned to the hotel, abandoning us to our karma. Mike told them our cabma worked out very well.

CHAPTER TWENTY-ONE

TURTLES ALL THE WAY DOWN

We passed the morning visiting old Xi'an's tangled streets and markets and the renowned T'ang Dynasty Great Mosque used by the Muslim Hui people of this region. We found it a peaceful temple in the Chinese style of flared cornices set in a serene garden. Unexpectedly, we could see right through the building, a lightness missed in generally gloomy Buddhist temples where statues and superstitious low ghost walls blocked the view. Then I remembered the Qur'an forbids icons.

I was surprised, therefore, to find outside the temple entrance an icon we had seen almost everywhere we visited in ancient China: a stone stela riding the back of a power-ful stone turtle, crowned at the top with a writhing stone dragon. I had expected the dragon—the Chinese, after all, are the dragon race, revering it as a symbol of strength and good luck—but I did not expect the Chinese universe to rest on the back of a turtle, my familiar.

In the northern Great Lakes region where I live, the Anishinabe (Ojibwe) creation story tells of a great flood, after which muskrat dove toward the bottom, finally bobbing to the surface with a fistful of mud. Placed on the turtle's back, that mud spread out to become the earth on which we live today. Gary Snyder famously titled his Pulitzer Prize–winning poetry collection *Turtle Island*, celebrating another of North America's many earthdiver origin stories.

I recalled the poet Charles Wright telling the famous Zen story as preface to his poem, "It's Turtles All the Way Down."

A student asked the Zen master, "Master, it is said the world rides on the back of a turtle. But Master, what does the turtle ride on?" "Another turtle," the master replied. After a pause, "Master, but what does that turtle ride on?" "Another turtle," the master answered again. After a longer pause, "My dear Master, then . . . " The master interrupted, exasperated. "It's turtles all the way down!"

"Yes," Bill said, "it's turtles all the way down, and dragons all the way up, wherever you go in China." I was feeling solidly at home on the Chinese turtle's back, if not under the dragon's smoky breath. It was time for us to turn from the bustling T'ang capital, where Cold Mountain once strived, toward the bedrock cave where he finally found home.

BOOK III

SLEEPLESS DREAMS TO
DREAMLESS SLEEP

CHAPTER TWENTY-TWO

GIVE IT ITS TRUE NAME

Bill had booked us "soft seat" berths on the over-night sleeper to Nanjing. We said good-bye to Mr. Chen and his Toyota van, now shrouded in thick layers of dust, thanking him profusely for his good karma. Then we hustled off toward the famously congested Xi'an train station.

Immediately caught in human gridlock at the station entrance, Mike wickedly whispered into my ear his personal etymology of travel: "From the Latin *trepalium,* 'mobile torture chamber,' related to the French *travail.*" Experienced travelers Margaret and Ed radiantly battled through the madhouse. Stuck on a jammed escalator, Margaret flashed a wide smile while Ed coolly disappeared to take photos throughout the packed waiting area. I felt a preternatural calm, like a paper boat floating down a river. Like most T'ang poets, we had tried our hand at the busy life of the capital. Now it was time to seek the solitude Cold Mountain sought.

Mike and I located our reserved sleeper compartment. A short, stout woman and her granddaughter already sat in the narrow room, booked on one upper and lower berth, we on the other. In an act of sweetness, Mike offered the stout woman his lower berth, via hand signals, as the top one looked difficult for her to scale, but she refused. With the child heaving mightily from behind, she clambered up and over. Mike climbed into his lower berth and immediately pulled down his eyelids. I settled in above him. The girl disappeared into a burrow of blankets in her bunk below.

As the train rumbled smoothly through the night like a wise old donkey that knows the way, I took out Bill's book of Cold Mountain translations and read them over one more time, despite a soundless television set flickering annoyingly over my head with no apparent "off" switch. At 11:00 p.m. the television suddenly went dark. I too went dark. I dreamed that a finger emerged from a Chinese embroidered robe and pointed harshly at a line of text: "Kid, give it its true name— Fire!" And, "Can he be a fraud, James? He had tears in his eyes."

Jolted awake, I scribbled the lines into my journal and fell back to sleep, the donkey rocking steadily below me, the words "fire" and "tears" ringing in my ears.

Awake in predawn light, I puzzled over the message in my notebook. For much of my life, I knew in my hands if not in my head that the interior life was my real work, and that reaching into it required the same heat of passion and discipline as did the practices of teaching, business, and journalism, my more remunerative trades. Poets forge the marriage of right sound and right sense in the furnace of desire. Only then can they strike the bell that reverberates around the world and over the drifts of time.

Perhaps I was not a boat afloat in a river of words after all, nor riding a passive donkey. I reminded myself that I did stay up all those nights writing and revising, got up early all those mornings writing and revising, though my only feeling was one of warm pleasure as I rubbed the flint of words together until my hands grew hot, tears the only evidence that I struck flame. And I climbed on this Chinese donkey myself, made it rumble and sway along the path toward Cold Mountain cave. Though I felt swept along, I rowed the boat, carved my own trail.

SLEEPING CAR NO. 10, XI'AN TO NANJING
The train sways, the car rattles, the faithful donkey pulls.
The stout woman in the upper berth snores,
her granddaughter disappeared under snug sheets.
My friend rasps dryly, a cold and sadness, missing his girl.
In my dream, a finger protrudes from a Chinese robe,
points harshly at a line of text:
"Kid, give it its true name—Fire!" And,
"Can he be a fraud, James? He had tears in his eyes."

CHAPTER TWENTY-THREE

MOON MUSIC

At dawn, the Nanjing train station was already a thick soup of humidity. In the parking lot, our new van driver, handsome Mr. Lin, gesticulated vigorously in the midst of an argument with a taxi driver over a newly bent fender. Bill had hired Lin to take us the rest of the way to Cold Mountain, then back to Shanghai for our departure. We were greeted as well by a tall slender American, Paul Hansen, a longtime Zen and poetry pal of Bill's from Port Townsend. Paul had moved to Nanjing to teach English and pursue his passion for translating ancient Chinese poems. Bill had invited him to spend the day with us as we visited memorials to Li Bai along the Yangtze River on the way to Cold Mountain. We happily jammed Paul's lanky frame into Mr. Lin's van, the squabble with the cab driver finally resolved, and our hundred horses turned south toward the wild country of Li Bai.

I was happy to be visiting one of the T'ang's most celebrated poets at the site where he famously drowned in the Yangtze attempting to embrace the reflection of the moon. That story is literary mythology, of course, but who doesn't love a poet's ecstatic desire for his metaphoric lover? His

most famous moonstruck poem is recited all over China to
this day.

Thoughts on a Quiet Night

Before my bed the light is so bright
it looks like a layer of frost
lifting my head I gaze at the moon
lying back down I think of home

(translated by Bill Porter)

Li Bai's seemingly effortless poetic musicality through
form, rhyme, and tonal play is music impossible to translate
and therefore music I will never hear. I thought of a moon
poem written by a young American friend of mine, Thorsten
Bacon, whose ear captures American moon music perhaps the
way Li Bai sings to Chinese ears.

Love Poem

Moon, moon!
MMM, our sound for deliciousness,
married with OOO, our sound for awe,
NNN, ending in such contentment—
the sound we make
falling back into the pillows again!

In the van we grilled Paul on his life story, and when he
mentioned he had been a friend of the North Dakota poet
Thomas McGrath, Mike nearly swooned. Mike made one of
his earliest documentary films about McGrath, *The Movie at
the End of the World*, an experience he told us felt like a "video

vision quest." Mike recited with a wide grin his "all-time favorite" McGrath poem, from *Letters to Tomasito*:

How could I have come so far?
(And always on such dark trails!)
I must have traveled by the light
Shining from the faces of all those I have loved.

Bill and Paul fell into a discussion of the problem of translation. Many of the ancient poets were "so allusive," Bill said. "Yes," Paul agreed. As he once wrote, "the almost endless references of a vast history and culture. . . . Hieroglyph inside hieroglyph—pictorial puns mirror sound, mirror meaning. . . . What is poetic communicates universal experience through the analogy of the particular; children, wandering, rivers, mountains, boats, crowds, separation, passion, monasteries, war and death." "Now even my own poetry is becoming that way," Paul added, "although I swore it would not. It's all about my life in China."

I recited to knowing laughter lines written by Sam Hamill sent to me years ago by poet Chase Twichell:

THE ART OF LITERARY TRANSLATION
Squabbling as they will
in busy traffic, two crows
make meals of road kill.

"Seems to me," I added, "that coming to China to translate poetry is like going to Saudi Arabia to drill for oil. There's an inexhaustible pool waiting to be brought to the surface. And when it arrives, it changes everything, including the infrastructure of one's own voice. It certainly has mine, and that from only a chance encounter with Cold Mountain, through Burton Watson and Gary Snyder. Pound, Bly, Wright, Merwin, all their voices were changed. And isn't *Letter to Tomasito* Tom McGrath's Chinese-inflected voice? Isn't that Chinese moonlight illuminating the faces of the family, friends, and poets he loved?"

As we relaxed into the remaining drive in silence, I sang my own moon song.

Moon Music

The moon laughs or cries, who really knows?
Old Li Bai knows, as if a golden gong, his golden song,
rings from the singing arc of ancient heaven.
Mother of months, mother of tides, mother
of fertile blood and moonstruck mating,
drunk on your shining, Li Bai sings
in tones of golden gongs I cannot hear,
and so I sing this slow sad sibilant song.

CHAPTER TWENTY-FOUR

DRINKING WINE WITH LI BAI

"This will be our first encounter with that long drink of water, the Yangtze, to which Li Bai has called us," Bill said from his front-seat perch next to Mr. Lin. "We look forward to spending the day with a friend." He told the tale that Li Bai's spirit flew up from the river to heaven on the back of a whale. More likely, Bill guessed, it was the back of a sightless Yangtze River dolphin that lived in this area until its probable extirpation due to the massive disruption of the Three Gorges Dam.

Said to have drowned in the moon's embrace, Li Bai didn't disappear, of course, but is preserved for eternity in his eleven hundred poems. The sightless and speechless Yangtze River dolphins weren't so lucky. On our short, pleasant boat ride on the river, we saw no sign.

To reach Li Bai's burial shrine, we bumped down a gravel road past a giant steel fabricating plant across from fields of smoking corn stubble. Arriving early at the empty parking lot, we noticed a red carpet rolled out from the shrine hall entrance to greet our merry band. Li Bai obviously anticipated our arrival. Alas, the royal greeting proved not for us. The ticket seller said "big head head" scholar-dignitaries from around the world were due soon for an international conference. A sign welcomed them in English: "A place for world historical scholars to end in." "We'd better move fast if we don't want to 'end' here like those scholars," Bill said.

Unlike the brooding, empathetic Du Fu, Li Bai was famous in his own time as a swashbuckling Byronic exotic who, tradition says, once folded poems into paper boats and floated them downriver. When he was first summoned to the court, the emperor honored him by seasoning his soup. Du Fu idolized the older poet for his fluid poetic gifts and wrote him admiring letters, an apparently unrequited epistolary relationship according to the historical record, although they wrote each other several poems.

This gravesite of Li Bai was memorialized a short sixty years after his death in 762. Walls surrounding the lush compound enfolded serene if not sun-spotted greenery, given the omnipresent haze. A pond waved with yellow lotus leaves. Willows trailed green fingers over the surface. A ludicrously romantic ten-foot-tall statue of Li Bai depicted him gazing devotedly upward toward his beloved wine cup, drinking alone with the moon.

> DRINKING ALONE WITH THE MOON
> I take my wine jug out among flowers
> to drink alone, without friends.
> I raise my cup to entice the moon.
> That, and my shadow make us three.
>
> But the moon doesn't drink,
> and my shadow follows silently.

Still, shadow and moon for companions,
I travel to the ends of spring.

When I sing, the moon dances.
When I dance, my shadow dances too.
Sober, we share life's joys;
drunk, each goes a separate way.

Constant companions although we wander,
we'll meet again in the Milky Way.
                    (by Li Bai, translated by Sam Hamill)

Inside the shrine hall, a freshly carved mural in bas-relief portrayed the poet standing heroically in the bow of his riverboat like a moonstruck George Washington crossing the Delaware. That pose might have pleased Li Bai, and would have made Cold Mountain howl with laughter until tears ran rivers down his cheeks.

In the quiet interior garden holding Li Bai's grave mound, we opened a bottle of wine purchased at the last minute at a nearby supermarket, a plastic-corked concoction made from sweet Concord grapes. We offered the first drink to Li Bai, pouring wine slowly down the granite face of his grave marker. "He's been thirsty a long time," Bill said. Then we toasted our host the way he would have toasted us, with poems and more wine. We bravely consumed the contents of the bottle, passing it back and forth as we sat on the steps and read aloud in both Mandarin and English poems Li Bai left us, from Bill's *Poems of the Masters*.

TRAVELING AWAY FROM HOME
The fine wine of Lanling with its turmeric scent
fills jade cups with its amber light
if only a host can keep his guests drunk
they'll soon forget about their hometowns

SEEING OFF A FRIEND
Dark hills stretch beyond the north rampart
clear water circles the city's east wall
from this place where farewell begins
a tumbleweed leaves on a thousand-mile journey
drifting clouds in a traveler's thoughts
the setting sun in an old friend's heart
as we wave and say goodbye
our parting horses neigh

Paul recalled his first visit eight years earlier to Li Bai's grave. To his surprise, he found it filled with ghosts of poet friends ancient and modern. Of course he wrote a poem about it, and read it to us. As he finished, he held the wine bottle high in comic imitation of the Li Bai statue, and melodramatically drained the last eleven drops. Just then the air filled with the chatter of arriving "big head head" scholars riding their red carpet on the legacy of Li Bai. We packed up and skedaddled just in time.

As we dropped Paul at the bus station for his return to Nanjing, our hearts neighed like Li Bai's horses at the departure of a friend.

CHAPTER TWENTY-FIVE

TWO DEPRESSING POEMS
IN WUHU

L i Bai is said to have spent his last years in the city of Wuhu, on the south bank of the Yangtze, because he admired the views. We spent one depressing night in a city that no longer sees the sky. We arrived so late the group decided to skip dinner, but Mike—a diabetic— needed to eat, so I accompanied him to the noisy street below our hotel. Past the clacking cacophony of an Internet café, we entered the first restaurant we found. The gold-toothed maître d' grinned when he saw us, and gestured us upstairs, which proved dark with young women selling favors. We bolted back to the street, raucous laughter trailing behind us. Surrounded by fumes and traffic clatter, we found a cluster of vendors selling street food—wontons charcoal-grilled on the cover of a fifty-gallon drum, two pennies a plate, large bowls of garlic chicken noodle soup, a penny a bowl, deliciousness at midnight on the Street of Good and Evil. Back in our room, we opened the window onto an acrid gloom through which the factory windows next door glowed with piece workers sewing clothing, the day shift sleeping on cots beside them.

We slept fitfully that night, the roar of buses, trucks, and two-stroke engines rattling the glass—and woke in a deep gloom we could taste. In this city of three million people where Li Bai once sang, it seemed everything useful for the bodies of the world was made, probably including the clothes we put on. The sun labored through smoke to understand. Once a month the full moon rose, mystified.

Departing early, Mike and I recited to each other two depressing poems, Mike's by Han-shan, the other by me. Mike calls Watson's translation "Bug in a Bowl."

COLD MOUNTAIN NO. 80
Man, living in the dust,
Is like a bug trapped in a bowl.
All day he scrabbles round and round,
But never escapes from the bowl that holds him.
The immortals are beyond his reach,
His cravings have no end,
While months and years flow by like a river
Until, in an instant, he has grown old.

BUG IN A POOL
What does the bug with the water wings know,
waiting to die in its air bubble?
What does it know of anguish?
What does the mud turtle learn from pain,
back half smashed by a tire, front half alive?
Do they curse, grieve, feel like failures?
As the iceberg melts five hundred miles at sea,
does the polar bear, stranded, scream?

I counted the remaining travel days ahead. We would spend tonight on a mountain blocking our way, because Bill insisted, then a night in Hangzhou. Then—finally—two full days in Tientai, as I insisted—one day to climb to the cave, one day to come down from whatever we might find there. I was growing impatient to arrive, beginning to miss the sunlight of home.

CHAPTER TWENTY-SIX

BEGINNING-TO-BELIEVE PEAK

B
ut as we rumbled south of the Yangtze for the first time, an entirely different landscape unfolded before us—a wet, rich country under blue skies. Rice straw shocks stood in bottomland fields like tiny tipis. Brushstrokes of dark tea bushes dotted the hillsides. Water buffalo grazed. Bamboo forests waved. Swaths of rice paper dried on open hillsides like drying bedsheets. Trucks transported long clumps of bamboo stalks like giant fishing poles. Distant mountains rose under dark conifer crowns. I had not expected conifers, my familiar. Bill said the area was famous for porcelain fired by local pine and cedar.

Our destination that morning was the most famous mountain scenery in China: Huangshan, Yellow Mountain, a World Heritage site. Bill insisted we not pass it by, as it was on our path, and had booked us rooms months in advance at a hotel built in a high valley.

Li Bai famously wrote of these mountains:

Thousands of feet high tower the Yellow Mountains
With thirty-two magnificent peaks,
Blooming like golden lotus flowers
Amidst red crags and rock columns.

(translator unknown)

Still, I was not at all prepared for what I saw when Mr. Lin turned off the narrow valley highway and ascended a steep side canyon, arriving in a parking lot already stacked with idling tour buses. Above us fantastic fingers of granite disappeared into layers of high, thick cloud. In all my years admiring traditional Chinese landscape painting—at the Minneapolis Institute of Arts, the Met in New York, the Nelson-Atkins in Kansas City, the Asian Art Museum in San Francisco—I had always presumed that the bizarre, fingerlike mountains rising in mist high above wandering poet-scholars were an imaginative trope, a range of fantasy mountains. At the base of the Yellow Mountains, I learned that they were real. "Fine-grained porphyritic granite from the Cretaceous with rare vertical as well as horizontal fractures," the guidebook said. I saw astounding columns supporting the cathedral of heaven.

A modern gondola whisked us three thousand vertical feet to the valley near the summit. Beneath us, trains of porters carried heavy loads dangling from bamboo poles up thousands of stone steps perhaps 1,500 years old. We disembarked into the ethereal landscape of those ancient paintings, with dark, hermit-like forms of weather-battered Huangshan pines wandering one by one into the distance.

ON FIRST SEEING THE YELLOW MOUNTAINS
Wild azaleas redden with envy at our autumn ascent
of the burnished granite peaks of Yellow Mountain.
Cable cars flying over stone stairs make our summit
easy.

Elegant dark pines shade our flimsy presence.
For a thousand years and more they've rooted
among these immortal views, melting granite for food.
Not even hermits or the Eight Immortals live up here.
Stone and pine and mist alone define this glimpse of
    heaven.

One of the porters, resting nearby, let me try to lift his
load, a bamboo pole with sacks of wet laundry suspended
from each end. He laughed as I staggered under the weight,
like lifting boulders.

We loaded on our flimsy backpacks and hiked the stone
trail to various spectacular view points, some reached by more
steps carved into the living rock. I admired the centuries-old
pines along the trail, some with individual names: "Dragon
Claw Pine," "Black Tiger Pine." All were *Pinus hwangshanensis*,
like our leader a species of durable red pine.

Our mountain hotel proved a squat, glassy tourist affair
snuggled against a forested slope, where we checked in and
caught a brief afternoon nap. Two hours before sunset, we
set out to climb to the topmost fingertip for a chance to see
the famous Huangshan sunset above the clouds. We rambled
up over giant boulders and carved stone steps, the steepest
ascents aided by heavy chains set into the granite like ropes.
The summit proved a bare field of crumbling granite not
much bigger than several quilts. A Chinese and an Australian
couple were already waiting with cameras on tripods to capture the sunset. We waited with them, sharing around our
bottle of Wanda red, toasting the granite under our feet, the

pines improbably rooted this close to heaven, and the sun in its wisdom above the clouds illuminating us all.

Back down in the noisy chaos of the hotel, we ate an indifferent tourist dinner much enlivened by the music of a lovely zither player. Bill got up and whispered a request into her ear. "Room 2408," he joked when he returned. His real request was the traditional song "High Mountain, Flowing Water." He told us the tale. A famous zither master would play only for himself, convinced no one could understand his music. One day a woodcutter passed by and overheard his music. "That sounds like high mountains," he said. The zither player changed his song, and the woodcutter responded, "That sounds like flowing water." They became inseparable friends. When the woodcutter died, the zither master smashed his instrument and never played again. In Mandarin today, the word for very best friend is *jur yin*, meaning "knows your tune," or "to know your tune."

I awoke in gray predawn light to a liquid song pouring three loud notes three times down the tonal scale: one, two, three, one, two, three, one, two, three. The bird sang only once, from somewhere in the forest outside our open window, but I was ready to answer the call. I dressed quickly and by 6:15 a.m. was hiking away from several tourist groups already milling about the hotel entrance, where guides with bullhorns prepared to lead them to see the famous Huangshan sunrise. The dawn here was said to be filled with "Buddha's light," though any visible sunrise this particular morning seemed unlikely given the low quilt of gray clouds and bursts of sputtering rain. As I followed the trail I read a tourist sign low to the ground: "Bright mountain flowers in full blossom arouse visitors inspiration and interest in sight-seeing. Please view and admire with cherishes." I remember everything about this day "with cherishes."

I followed a trail that led away from human chatter. I stopped only once, under an ancient pine, to listen to a slim brook murmur through a thin groove worn in the rock. I was jarred from my reverie by a sharp, taloned cry descending through the silent pine branches above me, and I hiked on. The boisterous crowd now well behind, I arrived at a prom-ontory named Beginning-to-Believe Peak. A lone squirrel scampered off. "Too crowded a place now," he thought, echo-ing the thoughts of this stranger from seven thousand miles away foolishly seeking the food of stillness in the remains of the world.

The trail ended on an anvil-shaped promontory projecting over a startling precipice. In the distance, thousand-foot stone columns marched gracefully away, fingertips dotted with thin brushstrokes of dark pine. Together they held up the arc of heaven. The familiar bark of a crow soared up from below, and I leaned out over the edge to catch sight of the bird. A for-est spread out below me, resembling soft green moss beneath my feet. As I leaned out as far as possible, guarded by links of a sturdy chain embedded in the rock, the clouds suddenly lifted their ruffled skirts and revealed the pink stripe of dawn. Then it vanished beneath gray skirts again.

Overwhelmed by the presences and absences around me, I sat down on a bench and opened my notebook. My pen's dark ink splashed in the spattering rain. Writing in a rush, lost in thought, I was startled by a sudden click of a stick behind me. I looked up into a vision. A beautiful woman, walking stick in hand, looked down upon me as I wrote. Nodding toward my pen and notebook, she trilled in English with a radiant smile, "Are you writing . . . poet?" "Yes, yes," I answered, grinning back up at her, more grateful than she could ever know for this annunciation.

FIVE BIRDSONG

At first light, a liquid trill: 1,2,3, 1,2,3, 1,2,3.
Only once, but I followed the call.
Under pines old as Chinese poets, I tracked dawn's
    chorus.
Pen in hand, I caught the caw of a soaring crow,
a hawk's scream through a canopy of shadows.
An angel landed quietly beside me on the trail.
"Are you writing . . . poet?" she twittered in my language.
"Yes," I warbled in gratitude, beginning to believe.

CHAPTER TWENTY-SEVEN

THE FLOATING WORLD OF
POET-ENGINEERS

Entering the exurbs of modern Hangzhou, we passed a string of shiny new auto plazas, the rewards of the new interstate highway system familiar to any American. Build it and they will come . . . to buy cars—and they have. China is now the third-largest car market after the United States and Japan (in 2011, China surpassed Japan, in 2012 America). At the city limits we passed yet another freeway under construction, supported by another mad filigree of bamboo scaffolding.

Hangzhou dazzled Marco Polo when he arrived here in the thirteenth century ("without doubt the finest and most splendid city in the world") and it dazzled us in the twenty-first. With a population of one or two million people back then, six or seven million today, the city radiates art and culture and economic progress. During the Song Dynasty, a period of relative stability after the collapse of the T'ang, woodblock printing and the invention of moveable type gave a tremendous boost to literacy, fomenting great leaps forward in science, engineering, and public administration, and creating a fertile ground for poets.

At 4:30 p.m. we arrived at our glass-fronted modern hotel overlooking West Lake, one of the most famous lakes in China. To me it resembled Lake Calhoun near my home in Minneapolis, a placid silver disc surrounded by tree-shaded hills, pedestrian walkways, and an automobile parkway punctuated with stately residences and pavilions, a serene respite near the heart of a thriving city. Across from our hotel, gondoliers waited at the docks with dragon boats to feast on tourists and lovers. We agreed we had to ride that dragon.

Bill negotiated the price, and just before sunset we gathered behind the good-luck gaze of our dragon prow, a bottle of Great Wall red wine in our talons. The rangy gondolier eased the boat past T'ang- and Song-era pagodas and pavilions lifting winged cornices through the trees, eaves lit with strings of white lights. As we rowed near a darkened pagoda on a forested island, its cornice lights suddenly snapped on. The oarsman laughed ruefully, saying the lights indicated a meeting of some "big big party officials" on the island. "Poor people never get to go there," he said. He oared on, passing a young couple in a punt reclined blissfully in each other's arms, unperturbed by our ghostly faces. We glided slowly toward the elegant stone archway of the Su Causeway, named for the poet Su Dongpo.

As governor of the Hangzhou region during the Song, Su Dongpo arranged for the rehabilitation of West Lake, clogged with centuries of sediment. He ordered the lake dredged and the construction of the pedestrian causeway that still bears his name, the one we were gliding under nearly a thousand years later. It is said he visited the lake daily, admiring it like a lover. He once wrote of this love affair:

Drinking on the Lake as It Clears Then Rains

The shimmering waves are translucent when it clears
the mist-veiled hills are transcendent when it rains
I think of West Lake as the Beauty of the West
equally lovely in powder or paint

(translated by Bill Porter)

Such an engineering achievement by a renowned poet thrilled me. In America, the idea of a poet-politician or poet-engineer seemed impossible, even absurd. Yet I grew up among poet-engineers. My father manufactured concrete products, including massive prestressed concrete bridge beams that could have easily spanned the Su Causeway and East and West Lakes. Civil engineers were the Apollos of my youth, admired throughout the factory where I worked every summer. Nothing made my father happier than to take the family to see the latest bridge built with his beams. I once wrote of that love.

Girders

I walk the river trail at sunset, the highway
vaulting over me and the river in twin sweeps.
I think of my father, who made heavy girders like these—
steady above me, beneath others, all safe.
I love, I see now, more than his boisterous laughter, his
tears.
I love the solid concrete and steel that remain,
girders resting delicately at the ends of long curved spans,
sheltering us all, and a dozen mud-daubed swallow's nests.

And my father loved poetry. He recited Chaucer's prologue to *The Canterbury Tales* and Robert Service's ballads to enthralled audiences throughout his college days at the University of Wisconsin. He wept with the sonnet sequence *Two Lives: A Poem*, published by reclusive university professor William Ellery Leonard in 1922, a heartbreaking tale of the mental breakdown and suicide of his wife. Dad recited the first lines of Leonard's introductory sonnet so often I too knew them by heart.

> The shining City of my manhood's grief
> Is girt by hills and lakes (the lakes are four),
> Left by the ice-sheet which from Labrador
> Under old suns once carved this land's relief,
> Ere wild men came with building and belief
> Across the midland swale.

In his restless retirement, my father cast those lines into a bronze plaque, which he fixed to a granite boulder—a glacial erratic—overlooking a waterfall he built at his church to please visitors, the residents of a nearby nursing home, and himself.

As we glided under the causeway, I thought of another hyphenated poet who changed my life, Senator Eugene McCarthy. His decision to run in the Democratic primary for president in 1968 against incumbent Lyndon Johnson electrified my generation, legitimizing our raucous effort to end the Vietnam War. My wife and I and our friends rode in caravans around the countryside, "clean for Gene," knocking on every door we could find.

I learned from Mike's 2003 documentary, *I'm Sorry I Was Right*, that McCarthy was a courageous poet as well as politician, one who could recite by heart his own poems and vast quantities of Yeats. Inspired by McCarthy the poet as well as the politician, I arranged what became his last public poetry reading, September 18, 2004 at the Loft Literary Center in Minneapolis. At eighty-eight, speech impaired from a recent stroke, eyes glittering, McCarthy struggled out a lifetime of pleasure in poetry before a packed auditorium. Dongpo would have admired McCarthy's courage.

COURAGE AT SIXTY
Now it is certain.
There is no magic stone,
No secret to be found.
One must go
With the mind's winnowed learning.
No more than the child's handhold
On the willows bending over the lake,
On the sumac roots at the cliff edge.
Ignorance is checked,
Betrayals scratched.
The coat has been hung on the peg,
The cigar laid on the table edge,
The cue chosen and chalked,
The balls set for the final break.
All cards drawn,
All bets called.
The dice, warm as blood in the hand,

Shaken for the last cast.
The glove has been thrown to the ground,
The last choice of weapons made.

A book for one thought.
A poem for one line.
A line for one word.

"Broken things are powerful."
Things about to break are stronger still.
The last shot from the brittle bow is truest.

Su Dongpo died August 24, 1101, at the age of sixty-four, during his second political exile. Eugene McCarthy died December 10, 2005, ending his long political exile during which he published more than a dozen books, three of them volumes of poems.

CHAPTER TWENTY-EIGHT

"SIX" AND THE SINGLE TRAVELER

Disembarking the dragon boat on the far side of West Lake at sunset, we walked to a lakeside restaurant for a dinner of stir-fried shrimp, vegetables, and beer, then strolled serene lakeshore paths back to the hotel. My friends drifted off to bed, but my tired feet called for a massage. I approached an attendant at the hotel spa and pointed to the photo on the wall of a foot soaking in a wooden tub next to the price of sixty-eight renminbi, about seven dollars, and gave him my hotel room number, as I had no cash. The attendant ushered me down a hall into a dimly lit room arrayed with a dozen divans. I was the only customer.

I lay down and arranged myself in relaxed anticipation. Above me two flat-panel televisions fired excited Chinese programs over my head, fortunately with the sound off. I closed my eyes against the visual din and immediately fell asleep.

"Six? Six?"

A strange high-pitched sound startled me awake.

"Six? Six?"

A young woman was sitting on my divan, speaking into my ear: "Six? Six?"

My befuddled mind wondered what "six" could possibly mean. I had agreed to sixty-eight renminbi. Was "six" sixty? Why less than sixty-eight? Did she want money now? I had none. I offered her multiple displays of incomprehension—shrugged shoulders, open palms, furrowed brow, lame smile. Finally she leaned close to my ear, clutched the inside of my thigh, and whispered in long, deep-toned English syllables: "Make looooove! Make looooove!"

I burst out laughing! "No, no, my dear," I said in consoling English, pointing at my feet. "*I really want a foot massage!*" But she was persistent, massaging her hand farther up my thigh, not toward my calf. I firmly removed her hand and pressed her cheeks with worn knuckles. "Go home, sweet girl," I said as gently as I could. "I am a father, a grandfather. I have daughters, a granddaughter. Go home to your family." Giving up, she flounced up off the couch in a cloud of teased hair and chiffon, and departed in a steamy huff. I shook my head. How my wife would laugh at me, naively believing a massage facility actually offered a massage! And how I grieved for this young woman, the life before her, her parents' dashed dreams. Prostitution is the world's second oldest profession, parenthood the first.

GRANDDAUGHTER LULLABY
When your childhood ends and dark street songs come,
and the spring in your feet leaves the ground,
I'll bring you the dreams of an elderly man—
my voice, and my hand, and my crown.

For the dreams of your youth and your sweet monkey-
    shines
turn my days and my nights into gold.
I love how strong and how dreamy you are,
and I'll never allow you to grow old, my dear,
never allow you to grow bitter and old.

A young man entered the room holding a wooden tub
filled with steaming water. He seated himself silently on the
hassock at the end of my divan, and gently pulled off one of
my shoes, then the sock. Then the other shoe, then the sock.
And for an hour or more he and his tub performed something like "six" on the soles of my feet. Now I was ready to
place one foot in front of the other up the southern slope of
Cold Mountain, no matter how far.

CHAPTER TWENTY-NINE

COLD MOUNTAIN: WHOSE STORY IS IT?

October 14, 2006, 6:15 a.m., the day
we travel to Cold Mountain

I spent a restless, anxious night, despite my contented feet, thinking about the day ahead. Mike and I both awoke before dawn. He tapped on his Macintosh while I scribbled in my journal. "I still have no idea how to give my gift," I said. "Give it to the current inhabitant," Mike responded.

I read again Watson's *Cold Mountain* translations, and read one out loud to Mike:

COLD MOUNTAIN NO. 38
Thirty years ago I was born into the world.
A thousand, ten thousand miles I've roamed,
By rivers where the green grass lies thick,
Beyond the border where the red sands fly.
I brewed potions in a vain search for life everlasting,
I read books, I sang songs of history,
And today I've come home to Cold Mountain
To pillow my head on the stream and wash my ears.

I noticed at the bottom of the page that my scrawled response was dated April 8, 1974. So I was thirty years old when I first came upon Cold Mountain's poems, the same age he was when he entered Cold Mountain cave—his wife and children gone, his original name lost, his solitary wonderings beginning.

My thirtieth spring, my wife and I were elbow-deep in cloth diapers for three chattering children while my job directing an alternative high school was dissolving me in stress. My thumb sprouted a cluster of warts to prove it.

That summer, I resigned my job, we moved to Minneapolis, I started a business, we found a house on a leafy street, our son loved the public school, and life's main questions were suddenly answered. In the quiet after the children slept, I watched my hand scribble at poems. Early in the morning I put them away.

Now half a life and half a planet away, our children fledged and flown, I was finally on the poet's journey, seeking the cave where I too could "pillow my head" and "wash out my ears." Watson wrote in a note to no. 38 that "washing of ears" referred to the "much older story of the sage recluse Hsü Yu, who, when asked by Emperor Yao to take over the throne, hastily went and washed his ears to cleanse them of such a vile suggestion." Yao was one of the legendary sage kings revered by Confucius as a model of selfless probity, the one Zhuangzi called the best of all men. How wise he was to offer power to one who had no desire to use it! How brilliant the response of Hsü Yu! How clear the stream!

I realized I too had been offered a throne, as the only son of a family business, and had spent much of my life scrubbing off its traces. I recited by heart to Mike the poem Watson placed first in his Cold Mountain story.

COLD MOUNTAIN NO. 1

My father and mother left me a good living;
I need not envy the fields of other men.
Clack—clack—my wife works her loom,
Jabber, jabber, goes my son at play.
I clap hands, urging on the swirling petals,
Chin in hand, I listen to singing birds.
Who comes to commend me on my way of life?
Well, the woodcutter sometimes passes by.

"I didn't realize it for decades," I said, "but that's my story too, in absurdly accurate detail. My wife's loom filled the living rooms of our first apartment and house. I loved to record my sons' jabbering voices. I plunge my nose into any fragrant flower I find, my beard covered with pollen. I'm even a bird listener! And I have that same mysterious longing for 'commendation.' Will a woodcutter ever pass by?"

SIXTY-TWO YEARS

Sixty-two years ago I entered this world.
I have traveled little, content to linger
near rivers and lakes where waters run clear.
Through wife, children, now grandchildren,
I have achieved immortality, no need to dream.

Now I read books I love, sing ancient songs.
Today I come to Cold Mountain to wash out
my ears, learn what clear ears can hear.

Back in the van, Mr. Lin's steady hands steered our horses onto yet another gleaming new freeway, this one headed toward the Tientai Mountains a three-hour drive ahead. As we rumbled south, I fell into a dreamless trance, fully waking only as we entered the tunnel to Tientaishan, the place Cold Mountain called home.

At the old town market, we paused to buy bananas and famous Tientai mandarin oranges. Then we drove the narrow road into the nearby mountains to which Han-shan's songs had called us.

CHAPTER THIRTY

THE HERMIT OF COLD MOUNTAIN

Wonderful, this road to Cold Mountain—
Yet there's no sign of horse or carriage.

HAN-SHAN

The pavement ended abruptly at a narrow bridge fording a rushing stream. Several children fished and played in the current, pantaloons rolled up. Beyond the bridge, a footpath wandered between shorn rice fields into a haze of azure mountains.

We climbed out of the van and pulled on our daypacks. "This is all new," Bill said, pointing to the concrete bridge and pavement under our feet. His first visit here, in 1989, took an hour and a half from Guoqing Temple, a backbreaking ride down muddy ruts on a powered rickshaw. That was the day he "discovered" the cave for American eyes. How did he find the way to Cold Mountain? He asked the monks at Guoqing. They pointed up the road, knew exactly where it was.

Pilgrims assembled, Bill led us across the bridge and onto the narrow trail, possibly the same one Cold Mountain walked all day to Guoqing back in the T'ang. Not a tall man, Bill moved surprisingly fast yet effortlessly and with good humor, befitting his decades of Zen practice. I am long-legged, in fine physical shape, a runner, yet found keeping his pace a challenge, one I loved to meet.

As we passed a resting cow and calf, Bill called out, "Do you know the way to Cold Mountain?" A mile or two up the trail, he pointed to a face of exposed cliff shining in southern sun. "That's Cold Mountain," he said, "or Cold Cliff, its other name." We could just make out, above trees that obscured our view, the wide, dark mouth of a cave entrance below a brow of sheer rock.

We turned up a red dirt trail toward the cliff, passing through a small orchard of dwarf fruit trees overhung with vines dangling volleyball-sized melons. A grove of green bamboo waved to us from the hillside where the trail met the cliff.

Suddenly, sharp cries rang out—a harsh, repeated chittering like the squeaking springs of an old car seat. Above us, two falcons pedaled the air before Cold Cliff's face, whirling out their alarm at approaching strangers. I did not need my field guide to identify them as peregrines. Like poetry, their cries are universal. Like pilgrims, they travel long distances—"peregrine" means wanderer. Like me, they mate for life.

With my binoculars, I watched them return to the cliff and settle onto a nest of sticks barely discernable in a crack above the eyebrow of the cave. They were satisfied, apparently, that the five approaching pilgrims did not pose a threat to their Cold Mountain home.

So few birds, so little birdsong, I thought, throughout our weeks of traveling through thickly populated, heavily

SEEKING THE CAVE

cultivated, gruesomely polluted China. Yet here, seven thousand miles from home, a familiar greeting. "The birds and their chatter overwhelm me with feeling" indeed.

At the cliff face, we climbed a hundred stone stairs to a wide floor before the cave entrance. The size of the opening surprised me, a huge crack rising from one corner of the cliff to the other in a sly jack-o'-lantern smile. A roofless brick dwelling was tucked into one side like a broken tooth. The rest of the wide, dark opening appeared empty. Bill ushered us through the raised mouth, and another song greeted us, this one high-pitched. "See that hole in the ceiling?" Bill asked. "Bats." More old friends! Every summer bat families lived in our bedroom wall, where we heard them nursing their babies and disciplining the teens that occasionally ventured inside the house instead of out.

In the dim recesses of the cave we could make out three sets of life-sized plaster statues painted dark red and clothed in crude robes and hats. Before them, incense sticks drifted fragrant dust from rough alters where a few votive candles flickered. "Looks like the locals now view the cave as 'Cold Mountain Temple,'" Bill said, noting an inscription painted on one wall. "Nobody accepted him in life. In death, they've apparently kicked him upstairs. That's how it goes in the Buddhist and Daoist universe." In poetry too, I thought, his twelve-hundred-year-old poems rough and fresh as handmade shrines.

Each shrine consisted of three crude figures. Bill identified the first grouping as representing Daoists, for one statue held pen and ink, another a book, signifying writing and the study of immortality. After carefully looking over the second and third groupings, Bill identified all of them with a smile as the three pals Cold Mountain, Pickup, and Big Stick. Cold Mountain smiled back at us under his signature birch bark hat.

As the others quietly drifted away to examine corners of the cave, I took from my backpack the handmade book of poems I'd carried all the way from the heart of America. I felt its lightness in my hands—the nearly transparent paper, the hand-sewn binding, the poems impressed with lead type that could be read by fingertips. I quietly thanked publisher Scott King for modeling this book on an ancient form that seemed to belong here. I thanked Han-shan, Cold Mountain, for carving his poems on bamboo and painting them on rocks and walls, and Lü Ch'iu-Yin for gathering them up into a book that gave them wings.

Once poems flap their way into the world, one can only watch them go, no idea where or when or if they will land. Han-shan's poems fluttered into my life from twelve hundred years and seven thousand miles away. Not far. Not far at all.

I quietly recited a Han-shan song, placed the book, my response to Han-shan's call, at the foot of one of his three shrines, then stepped back through the cave mouth toward suddenly abundant sunlight.

Then we had lunch, with the current hermit of Cold Mountain.

She crested the steps just as we were departing, her thin frame stooped under a broad-brimmed hat and shoulder-load of firewood. Her radiant smile insisted we stay. In the

SEEKING THE CAVE

roofless brick room inside the cave, she wordlessly set out on a rough wooden table bottles of warm beer, rice, homemade pickles, cucumbers, carrots, chunks of mushy melon, and very strong—possibly off—tofu. She ate with us, smiling broadly and nodding, her face lined like an ageless shrine. "She may be a Buddhist," Bill said. "When I mentioned a famous monk, she rocked back and forth, rolling her eyes with delight."

After lunch we offered her our own delighted smiles and bows of gratitude. She smiled radiantly again, as if the sun lived in this cave. As she turned to clear away some dishes, Bill slipped a banknote under the pickle dish, guessing that dish would be the last she would pick up. Then he urged us to scuttle over the rim of the cave quickly to the valley below. "Otherwise," Bill said, "when she finds the money she'll run after us to return it. That's the way it is with hermits. They'll give you nothing but everything they have."

Locals had told Bill she appeared about five or six years ago. No one knew her name. No one knew where she came from. And she didn't speak. "I call her Butterfly Woman," Bill said, "because she smiles a lot." I'll call her Cold Mountain.

CHAPTER THIRTY-ONE

"THE BIRDS AND
THEIR CHATTER"

Five quiet pilgrims entered the gates of Guoqing temple that afternoon, our final stop on Cold Mountain's trail. Guoqing (pronounced *Guo-ching*) is the same temple where Cold Mountain visited his pals Pickup the kitchen helper and Big Stick the monk back in the T'ang. The several hundred monks resident here were quite used to foreign pilgrims, so our arrival made no stir.

Bill sent a message to the guest manager, and while we waited in an interior courtyard we observed hired farmers swat at grain on the courtyard floor with long-handled flails and turn the crank of an old wooden rice-hulling machine. Gray-robed monks shoveled the finished rice into woven baskets big as barrels, then dragged them off to winter storage. The air whirred with busy harvest activity.

The guest manager strode up wearing a light gray tunic and wrapped leggings. He conversed briefly with Bill, an old friend, then hustled us through two more interior courtyards and up several flights of stone stairs. He nodded toward two rooms down an airy corridor and was gone. "He is very efficient," Bill said. "He's also a poet. He is happy we've brought poets here."

Mike and I dropped our bags in a large room with open windows overlooking a courtyard centered on an immense camphor tree with a thick green crown. Bill told us a second courtyard held a plum tree believed to be the oldest cultivar in the world, from the sixth century, when the temple was founded. "Botanists haven't been able to find any older. But the Chinese love to exaggerate."

Densely forested hills sheltered the temple complex, six hundred rooms in fourteen different halls, and the monastery owned additional land on the valley floor, source of the rice harvest. Why, I asked Bill, was Guoqing Temple not destroyed in the Cultural Revolution along with so many others? "Even in the maddest Communist heyday some temples had powerful friends," Bill said. "Remember, this is the founding temple of Chinese, Japanese, and Korean Buddhism when it broke from Indian Buddhist tradition, forging its own path. The oldest wall dates from 598 CE."

For dinner that night we walked to a new hotel nearby that Bill had read about. Out the temple gate, we hiked up a cobblestone road under a thick overhang of forest. A song of rich, repeated phrases cascaded over us from the forest's upper story. I lingered awhile in its presence.

The hotel surprised us, a shiny box of glass and stainless steel set in the deep forest, a Ka-ching shock next to the terra-cotta gravitas of the temple. The fidgety maître d' appeared pleased to see customers, even scruffy, bearded barbarians. He gave us a table covered in a white tablecloth, the first we had seen in quite a while. We selected dinners not from plastic menus but from lavish displays of dishes set out on four long tables, and a bubbling aquarium teeming with crabs, fish, and eels. We turned down snake, but enjoyed crab custard, rice balls with meat, potatoes in hot peppers, two mushroom dishes, fried egg rolls, and numerous beers.

While we ate, Bill told the story of his travels in this region during the democracy protests of 1989. "Those months were national euphoria," he said. "The entire nation felt like it was on holiday. Every day was Chinese New Year. Then it was over. Like that.

"Now the government loves Buddhists," Bill continued. "They don't stir up politics, only compassion and meditation. Since the end of the Cultural Revolution, there's been an explosion of Buddhist practice and monastic life."

All that human energy had to go somewhere, I thought— Buddhism flowering in caves and temples, business booming everywhere else in the Ka-ching. With carbon emissions ravaging the global climate, the timing for a radically enlarged Buddhist practice could not be more propitious; the timing for Western-style energy consumption could not be worse. But that argument was for another time, another place. What could I possibly have said to today's Chinese, a visiting American with generations of carbon footprints behind every step I took?

As we left the hotel, we overheard a woman arguing loudly with her taxi driver, bitterly slamming the car's front door. Straightening her teased hair and pulling an ill-fitting satin coat around her, the young woman wobbled on too-high heels toward the lobby entrance, probably a "six" worker reporting for duty. "She may have been angry because the driver asked for 'additional favors.' There's AIDS in China,"

Bill said. She was too thin. We walked somberly down the hill, serenaded by roadside crickets.

I awoke the next morning to a cacophony of birdsong flooding through the open, sunlit window. I leaned out to see a hundred white-headed black birds noisily flapping on their roost high in the crown of the camphor tree. Their boisterous chatter overwhelmed me with feeling. The birds—bulbuls, according to my field guide—were nearly as loud as the flock of Buddhist pilgrims that soon entered the courtyard to pay their respects at the central shrine.

After breakfast we strolled outside the front gate to visit market stalls set up along the temple entrance road. I found an antique platter glazed with cobalt I knew my wife would love. I decided to buy it, knowing I would have to carry it carefully in my arms the rest of the trip. I was beginning to long for home.

Late that afternoon, as the din of daily pilgrims subsided, Mike, Bill, and I sat together in the deepest recesses of the temple grounds, a wooded hillside rising behind us, dragon cornices receding down the hill below. Bill read out loud several Cold Mountain poems in both Mandarin and English, and we talked about why this poet had drawn us here.

A pungent observer of a literate society much like ours, Cold Mountain was an ordinary man, probably a lay Buddhist at the end of his life. Like almost all educated men of his time, he sought a job in the empire's bureaucracy, banging his head against the civil service exam more than once. "A blind boy aiming at the eye of a sparrow / Might just accidentally manage a hit."

We know from his poems that he had a brother, married,

fathered at least one son. He rode a white horse—like driving a Porsche convertible these days—and lived in the capital. Somehow he lost it all, probably as a result of the catastrophic An Lushan Rebellion, and retired alone to Cold Mountain cave. He lived off what that small world, and this nearby temple, gave him in friendship, food, and birdsong. In return he wrote a few poems, laughed a lot, and meditated on the conundrum of existence. Had it not been for Lü Ch'iu-Yin, who gathered his poems from rocks and trees and village walls into a book, he would have remained forever unknown, one of millions of poets like him.

My mind wandered along my own Cold Mountain path. I had completed an improbable pilgrim task that had first called to me in a tiny bookstore in Western Massachusetts more than thirty years ago. Since then, Han-shan's songs had only grown louder, yet ever more intimate and familiar, like the voice of an older brother whispering in my ear.

My mother's voice drifted into my mind. She had been eighty-five, maybe ninety, speaking with that rare edge of tremolo she used when intent on communicating something truly important, a fact of life. There had been an older brother, she said. Her first pregnancy. She felt she had been too tense, too nervous, she blamed herself. No time, no marker, the next three healthy, two girls, and me the last, and life. As this forgotten memory flowed back into me now, the memory of her lost child had never left her, something important she wanted me to know before my sisters, my wife, and I sang her into heaven at ninety-five.

I realized now that an older brother had been my

companion, that presence and absence, my entire life, the wise and funny voice I heard in Han-shan's songs. The first-born son called to the second born to become myself: neither businessman—expectation for a firstborn—nor even teacher or journalist, tasks eagerly assumed along the way, but a man in love with the riddle of sound and sense.

GRATITUDE TO THE POET OF COLD MOUNTAIN
When I first heard your voice, tears coursed down my
    cheeks—
of memory for what I did not know I'd lost,
an older brother beneath our backyard apple tree,
the Fox River flowing by named for a forgotten people.
I climbed those branches as a boy in search of
    the delicious.
Today, seeing you sweetly robed in red, named and
    nameless,
remembered in a forgotten place, I sing your songs
as birds sing night and day in apple-laden branches.

I thought of my wife, who saw me correctly from the beginning as I did not, from the first moment she cast her fiery eyes upon me at a raucous college party, not as a first son in disguise but as a second son whose letters made her laugh, whose poems made her cry.

ONCE IN THE SIXTIES
    after William Stafford
I favor shirts the color of mustard and blood, she only
    white or blue.

Why then did she choose me across a room crowded
    with white and blue?
Was it that I stood alone, wearing sideburns and a
    crimson jacket?
I saw in her eyes oceans where migrating salmon swim
    toward home,
her knees so white hot they seared me against any other
    world but this.
Now as I duck out the door in my cinnamon shirt to
    write short poems,
she, dressed in her long black robe, sends to newspapers
    her flaming prose.
All the good of my life began with this still disturbing
    affliction.

I recalled a poem by Juan Ramón Jiménez, translated by
Robert Bly.

I Am Not I

I am not I.
                    I am this one
Walking beside me whom I do not see,
Whom at times I manage to visit,
And whom at other times I forget;
The one who remains silent when I talk,
The one who forgives, sweet, when I hate,
The one who takes a walk where I am not,
The one who will remain standing when I die.

I thought of Robert Bly himself, whose poems and translations changed the ear of American poetry from a kitchen
table on a farm on the Minnesota prairie. Who later moved
to Minneapolis and became my neighbor, then my friend.
Robert's elder brother, the firstborn, lived and died a hard-
drinking, row-crop farmer like their father. So that Robert,
the second son, could be forgiven when he drove the tractor
off the far edge of the field as a boy, lost in thought memorizing the music of the *Rubáiyát of Omar Khayyám*. Like Jia Dao,
he was allowed to cultivate the poet's path, not forced to wear
a father's coveralls that did not fit.

A few years ago I wrote this poem.

My Father

Loved me, from before I was born to the day he died—
this son who would carry his happy name through time.
His first son dead, and so this second, the shy, sickly one,
with shoulders built of thin, protruding bones.
I feel him now looking over my shoulder,
tears streaming down his cheeks. Of happiness
I always thought, not knowing he remembered
    another son
with small sturdy shoulders buried in the garden.

I remembered the moment Robert Bly nudged me along
the poet's path. At the first reading of my Han-shan-style
collection, *Han-shan Is the Cure for Warts*, Bly sat in the front
row with his wife, Ruth. I was especially eager for him to
hear "Glacial Erractic," my vision of the artist in the world.

GLACIAL ERRATIC

In the fields of Wisconsin, rocks with no other names
fill cairns like hills where each was hauled.
Pieces of the distant north, carried here by ice,
buried by ice, moved one last time by human hands.
And still every spring surprises push up.
One of them is you, the other me.
Outliers. Annoyances. Placed in a joyous heap
Around which all the straight, important work gets done.

When I read the last line, Bly winced, a shudder that entered
my heart like a knife. I was deeply proud of these poems. Had
lovingly set the type by hand. Had spoken exuberantly to the
audience about what had transpired in my writing life since
leaving the *Star Tribune*, now with the astonishing prospect of
Cold Mountain cave before me. Yet I was still withholding my
commitment to the poet's path. "Straight" work still felt more
"important" than the work of that "joyous heap" of outlier artists. That line was my father's business voice, not the voice of the
poems he and I loved. I was not yet worthy of the name "poet."

That spring I traveled to the far northwestern corner of
Minnesota, scratching the North Dakota and Canadian bor-
ders, to write an article about the abundant local wildlife. My
guide, naturalist, photographer, and friend David Astin surprised me by stopping his van near a glistening, newly plowed
field. He pointed to a large rock cairn in the center of the field,
built by generations of farmers picking rock after rock after
spring thaws pushed them up into the path of the plows. David
knew "Glacial Erratic" by heart. He urged me to stand on the

cairn for a photograph, so I jogged out across the furrows to climb the stones.

I had been working hard at poems and manuscripts since leaving the *Star Tribune*, slowly beginning to believe, not just in poems, but in the vocation of poet. When I stood on top of the cairn in the center of that flat field in golden early morning light, I recognized for the first time that the sturdy artistry of the cairn influenced the entire flow of the field, the way a boulder in a stream influences the stream, the way a painting or sculpture changes the look of the landscape. Like the biggest bell in the world, a work of art vibrates farther than we can hear.

When I republished "Glacial Erratic" in the trade edition *A Cartload of Scrolls: 100 Poems in the Manner of T'ang Dynasty Poet Han-shan*, I made a small correction that changed everything: "around which all straight work eventually must bend."

A RARE QUIET SETTLED over the temple grounds. Then another song lifted from the thick woods up the hill behind where we sat. Faint at first, barely perceptible, it built louder and louder until it echoed through the reverberate hills. Not birdsong, nor bat nor cricket, but a high-pitched, penetrating keening.

The song arced slowly back and forth, lifting and receding, filling the valley of the temple between the mountains behind and the mountains ahead, as if the hills themselves were vibrating with song. "The character for 'cicada' is the character for 'Zen' plus the character for 'bug,'" Bill said. "Zen bugs."

Final Sound at Guoqing Temple

After the tide of noisy pilgrims withdraws, cicada song,
the long arc of their longing pitched high as the bowl of
   sky.
So that is the song ringing in my ears—tinnitus, the
   doctors say.
I have no choice but to listen, night and day.
Out of the ground I crawled, up the rough bark of an
   ancient tree.
At sixty-two, nearer the crown than the roots, I pause,
rub my bones together, and wait for your reply.

Inside all of us there is singing. My own song grew loud
enough for me to hear it these last few years, my Confucian
responsibilities fulfilled as best I could. Now I knew what
that song was. Zen bugs. Living poems.

Steady Work

Steady work, this poetry.
Every night, late, or every morning, early,
with the busy world settled to a forgotten dot or hum.
No sense saving it up, there's always more.
The dark well has no bottom, the dark sky boundless
   space.
No wages, but no cost. A bit of ink, a scrap of paper,
courage to climb down, wings to slowly rise.

CHAPTER THIRTY-TWO

THE NUN'S PRIEST'S TALE

Now it is that, straying from the path,
You ask your shadow, "What way from here?"
HAN-SHAN

The next morning we said good-bye to Guoqing Temple, its chanting monks, its visiting pilgrims, its portly abbot who entertained us at tea under his window air conditioner, its efficient house manager who quietly slipped Bill a poem, its Zen bugs. On the way out we bought a few souvenirs from monks at the temple store, where the monastery earned needed cash. In the distance other monks chanted musical sutras, others slapped rice.

As Mr. Lin threaded the van out the gate and past the street vendors again setting up their stalls, I looked back at the forest-sheltered walls so full of song. The monk Feng-kan lived here during the T'ang. The foundling Shih-te was raised here. The hermit Han-shan waited in the kitchen for table scraps. I visited from America. We all heard the same song.

In the Ka-ching Dynasty, some monks answer cell phones. Others sit under an office air conditioner or chant before ten thousand gleaming statues of Buddha. Yet they all take in pilgrim wanderers every day. They center the body and seek the spirit by launching poetic songs toward the heavens. And they maintain an oasis where Zen bugs wash our ears of the illusion that our songs are not, in the end, immortal.

That lesson was more than enough for me. I was ready for home. But Bill had one more surprise for us on Cold Mountain's trail.

I'd assumed Mr. Lin would take the freeway directly back to Shanghai for our departure early the following day from Pudong Airport. Instead, following Bill's directions, we meandered a narrow road flanked on one side by a sheer rock cliff, on the other by green fields planted right to the tarmac. We scraped through a single-lane tunnel crudely carved through a rock outcrop, then turned into a compound of buildings nestled at the entrance to a narrow box canyon.

Baffled, we stepped out of the van and followed Bill into the nearest building. It was new and sparsely furnished, a dusty cash register idle at one end of an empty glass counter, a few brightly painted Buddha sculptures seated on the other. Suddenly the room erupted in a burst of elation as a Buddhist nun entered and rushed toward Bill, her gravelly voice brimming with enthusiasm like meeting an old friend. Bill hadn't told us, but he'd met her once before on a visit to this place, when there was no paved road, only a ragged trail to the crack in the mountain.

This was the spot, according to legend, where Cold Mountain disappeared. T'ang official Lü Ch'iu-Yin was the source of the tale. After Han-shan ran away, laughing wildly, refusing to accept Lü's obeisance, Lü sent out packers to bring him gifts to honor his reputation as a healer and bod-hisattva. The tale continues, as translated by Gary Snyder:

> The packer saw Han-shan, who called in a loud voice, "Thief! Thief!" and retreated into a mountain cave. He shouted, "I tell you man, strive hard!"—entered the cave and was gone. The cave closed of itself and they weren't able to follow. Shih-te's tracks disappeared completely.

The enterprising nun had colonized the location, and as abbot was constructing a nunnery using Cold Mountain's story as the fuel for her dreams. She announced proudly, Bill translating, that she had five nuns in residence already! She refused to allow us to pay the entrance fee and instead grabbed two of us energetically by the arms and launched us on a tour of her realm. As she showed off the sights, she waved her arms wildly above her shaved head and gray tunic. Her enthusiasm—*en-theos*, from God—reminded me of my father in one of his many bouts of civic boosterism, and me in my own. In her new shrine hall she proudly showed off a new sculpture of the Cold Mountain pantheon: Han-shan, Feng-kan, and Shih-te. Unlike the rustic chipped and scarred plaster versions in Cold Mountain cave, hers were freshly carved wood with bright paint and happy smiles. She planned to use them to greet her flood of future visitors.

As we followed her deeper into the canyon, she pointed out real and imagined treasures. Down there was a newly constructed pond where the nuns would soon raise fish to eat. Up above it, a massive rock seventy feet high leaned against the cliff face. Gesticulating mightily, she attempted to convince her skeptical audience that the rock and cliff together created an image of "praying hands." Then she pointed to a second boulder, which she said looked "exactly" like an image of the Buddha, though again none of us could see it.

We walked higher through moss-covered greenery toward the box end of the narrow canyon. She stopped dramatically at a particular spot. One by one, she took us each by the arm and insisted we look up. High above, where the rocks joined together into a sheltering arch overhead, a tiny hole remained open to the sky, and sunlight poured through it like starlight. "That's it!" she exulted. "That's what?" Bill asked. "The daylight star! The place where Cold Mountain disappeared!"

Back at the van, she pressed sweet mandarin oranges into each of our palms, including one for Mr. Lin. We thanked her, and quietly left her bills, certain her nunnery would prosper.

Who is to say the poet called Cold Mountain didn't become a Buddhist? Or a Daoist? Or an older brother? Or a daylight star?

CHAPTER THIRTY-THREE

ONE NEW GOD

Mr. Lin threaded our way back to the freeway for the five-hour drive to Shanghai and home. Along the way, we whispered to each other our newest amazements, then fell into individual meditations. It occurred to me that, remarkable as the abbot of the nunnery was, it had been Lü Ch'iu-Yin who did what was truly important. After Han-shan and Shih-te disappeared, here's his story, again in Gary Snyder's translation:

> I ordered Tao-ch'iao and the other monks to find out how they had lived, to hunt up the poems written on bamboo, wood, stones, and cliffs—and also to collect those written on the walls of people's houses. There were more than three hundred.

He bound them into a book.

No one knows for sure if the Cold Mountain tale is true, or even if Lü Ch'iu-Yin was who he said he was. No record exists of a high official with that name in the Tientai region at that time. But the book of poems he compiled, or wrote, or others fabricated or elaborated, found its way to Japan and Korea, and now to America.

I learned on this trip that the Chinese don't much care for Cold Mountain's poems—his rough, colloquial voice, his uncertain, eccentric ways. China will always be a Confucian nation, orderly and disciplined, as the world is fast relearning today. The Japanese are much more interested in poet-eccentrics, and they studied and preserved Cold Mountain's poems until Waley, Snyder, Watson, Red Pine, and others brought him to American ears, where his voice has become our familiar.

Perhaps Cold Mountain is the older brother America never had.

In his introduction to *Translations from the Chinese*, Arthur Waley wrote, "The poems in this book are by poets whom the Chinese themselves have always greatly admired. I have not attempted to set up any new gods." He did not include Cold Mountain in that collection. But soon enough, in 1954, he published twenty-seven Cold Mountain translations in *Encounter* magazine, the first in what has become a long line of English versions, and a new poetic god began to sing in English. In China, Han-shan became a Buddhist bodhisattva and Daoist immortal worthy of a shrine; in America, a healing poet worthy of a visit.

LEN-FESTE'S SHRINE

My Cold Mountain is the mouth of the cave itself.
Its statues the pillars of song holding the door forever open.
Its chants the calls of bats, cicadas, anxious falcons.
Its votives the rays of morning sun kissing the cave's lips.
Its worshipers the ones who stumble into a bookstore
    far away,
sick at heart, warts covering their hands, seeking a poem
    to cure them.

CHAPTER THIRTY-FOUR

MEANWHILE, BACK IN
THE KA-CHING

Now I face home again, very pleas'd and joyous,
(But where is what I started for so long ago?
And why is it yet unfound?)

WALT WHITMAN, "FACING WEST FROM

CALIFORNIA'S SHORES"

Shanghai, like Alice on magic cake, grows and grows and grows. "It's the economy, stupid," smart people say these days, and the economic cake clearly tastes sweet to the hundreds of millions of Chinese already pulled from poverty in less than thirty years, an economic miracle unprecedented in human history. The impressive freeway approach to Shanghai carves a trail through a twenty-mile forest of high-rise apartment complexes, like stands of redwoods. We finally reached the booming heart of the city of thirty million for a last night at a hotel on the famous Bund on the bank of the Huangpu River, the new city of Pudong soaring from a former swamp on the other side.

After dinner, we strolled the lovely quay, agreeing the temperature was perfect, unable not to marvel at the massive LED and neon displays flashing up the spines of towering high-rises across the river and riding the backs of river barges like fiery dragons, a Ka-ching excess rivaling the Ginza and Times Square. In our hotel room that night, Mike and I were kept awake by the hoots of barges busily passing on the river below. I eventually fell asleep, for I awoke in the throes of an intense and involved dream. I was part of a throng attending a large wedding celebration of Native American friends. As we waved tearful good-byes to the bride and groom and the wedding party, their departing cars suddenly accelerated toward the freeway at insanely high speeds. One car lifted off a rise in the pavement and landed upside down, bounced, rolled over, and careened into roadside trees, followed by another car, then another. We stood frozen in horror as the wedding vehicles rocketed away, unable even to scream.

DEPARTING FRIENDS AT PUDONG AIRPORT
Already my mind is home.
I see myself placing gifts on the kitchen table,
allowing her to choose her favorites,
laugh at the rest.
Then shower and sleep, no more dreams.

All night the Big Dipper rode with our 747, arm in arm. I drank two Sapporos but still could not sleep. At dawn, the featureless abyss of the Pacific greeted me out the window. As we began our descent toward Seattle's Sea-Tac

Airport, the plane was suddenly illuminated by an intense, fiery light, the way Cold Mountain disappeared into his mountain crag. The daylight star! Then the plane plunged into a blanket of thick cloud. Its windows ran with tears of healing rain.

EPILOGUE

CHRISTMAS MORNING

CHRISTMAS MORNING 2006

In Seattle, winter dark lingers long.

Grandchildren skitter upstairs, enjoined to wait till eight.

I make coffee, read a chapter of *Soul Mountain*.

"Times of peace and prosperity are rare indeed," writes
    Gao Xingjian.

Two boys, sick last night from cookie dough, dance
    excitedly,

our daughter and son-in-law exhausted by reindeer
    drumming the roof.

Before all and after all, stillness. Before eagerness, after joy.

Now let the children descend, let the grateful applaud.

POSTSCRIPT

FINDING MY OWN TRUE NAME

Drink, Pilgrim, here! Here rest! And if thy heart
Be innocent, here too shalt thou refresh
Thy spirit, listening to some gentle sound,
Or passing gale or hum of murmuring bees!

SAMUEL TAYLOR COLERIDGE,

"INSCRIPTION FOR A FOUNTAIN

ON A HEATH"

Why did Bashō embark for the Far North? To experience at every turn the journey, and if lucky find a poem or two along the way.

I found poems too, in my journal when I returned, and also stories—the first of the journey itself and, over the years of writing this book, a second story, of the journey inward.

I had been able to rearrange my life, a difficult and fraught process, to honor the call of Han-shan's songs. I learned that Cold Mountain is real. She wears a broad-brimmed straw hat over a radiant smile, and a nun's cassock under a daylight star. That was joy and surprise enough.

But I also learned my own true name: *poet*, one I had resisted my entire life, feeling the artist's path unworthy, and me unworthy of that path. I am happy now, like Cold Mountain, to paint my poems on rocks and trees, like Li Bai to ink them on paper boats, like millions of unknown poets to carve them on the crumbling shoulders of mountains, float them down the river of time, flutter them on kites like butterflies into timeless skies.

POETRY AND BIRDSONG
Poetry and birdsong: who understands either one?
Like a mad dream, they wake us up!
Passionate calls from a high branch,
mutterings from a dark cave of cedar.
In the velvet suspicion of first light,
before children wake and the dawn bell clangs,
ears open to these mysterious sounds, and
you weep for your life, the incomprehensible joy of it.

I returned too with a sense of finding something I hadn't known was lost. No more "one / walking beside me whom I do not see." No more yearning for "commendation" for a life not my own. Now my whole body is singing. The woodcutter passed by, put down her saw for a moment, and listened.

WANG WEI'S ADVICE
Want to know how to avoid sick old age?
All you do is study how not to be born.
Wang Wei
I did not meet you on the trail, Wang Wei,
but textbooks for your study cobbled my path.

My older brother, Not Born, thus not an older brother.
Cold Mountain, maybe Not Born, leading my way.
Wind and waves are voices of the Not Born.
They are happy where they are.
Why can't the born say the same?
Wang Wei, I have learned how to be Not Born.

Finally, I found one other name that fits me, and fits us all—*pilgrim*. I learned I am but one more seeker of caves climbing far older stone stairs one at a time, reciting even older poems the way bats chatter to their children, falcons warn away strangers, and cicadas speak their love: nature's speech. It is a journey from beloved community to beloved solitude and back again. I returned the same man but different—beard a bit longer, eyes wilder yet calm, heart comforted by its steadfast decision to depart, ears by what they heard along the trail. I took the left-handed path into distant mythological mountains, and safely returned. Now I am fully home.

I HAVE TRAVELED ENOUGH
I have traveled enough in this world.
I have heard the eternal cicada's song—
language of the temple, the court, the heart.
Now wherever I travel, there I am.
When I sit, my mind sits too.
When I dance, the air around me whirls.
When I die, I feed the earth that fed me.

NOTES

xi *There is only one way*   Sheila Erwin, "From the Interior Outward: A Talk with Poet Jane Hirshfield," *The Bloomsbury Review*, May/June 2006.

PROLOGUE

xvii *"Letter to James Wright"*   Robert Bly, "Letter to James Wright," *Great River Review*, Spring/Summer 2010, 90.

xvii *Here we languish*   Han-shan, *Cold Mountain: 100 Poems by the T'ang Poet Han-shan*, trans. Burton Watson (New York: Grove Press, 1962), 28. Charles Miller later wrote a fine memoir about his own mentor, *Auden: An American Friendship* (New York: Scribner, 1983).

xix *Men ask the way*   Gary Snyder, *Riprap and Cold Mountain Poems* (San Francisco: Four Seasons Foundation, 1958), 42.

CHAPTER ONE

4 *"a chronicle of spiritual search"*   Han-shan, *Cold Mountain: 100 Poems*, 14.

7 *I reflect that man*   Burton Watson, ed., *The Columbia Book of Chinese Poetry: From Early Times to the Thirteenth Century* (New York: Columbia University Press, 1984), 77.

CHAPTER THREE

19 *Cold Mountain no. 85*   Han-shan, *Cold Mountain: 100 Poems*, 103.

20 *Do you have the poems*   Ibid., 118.

21 *Nothing in the cry*   Matsuo Bashō, *The Poetry of Zen*, trans. Sam Hamill and J. P. Seaton (Boston: Shambhala, 2004), 150.

CHAPTER FOUR

24 *Ryōkan no. 35*   Ryōkan, *Ryōkan: Zen Monk Poet of Japan*, trans. Burton Watson (New York: Columbia University Press, 1977), 94.

24 *Ryōkan no. 259*   Ibid., 101.

25 *Who says my poems are poems?*   Ibid., 11.

CHAPTER SIX

37 *Summer grasses*   Bashō, *The Poetry of Zen*, 136.

37 *The whole country*   Tu Fu [Du Fu], *The Poetry of Zen*, 136.

45 *In Xanadu*   Samuel Taylor Coleridge, *The Complete Poetical Works of Samuel Taylor Coleridge*, ed. Ernest Hartley Coleridge (Oxford: Oxford at the Clarendon Press, 1912; Project Gutenberg, 2009), 297. http://www.gutenberg.org/ebooks/29090

48 *And he had been the first*   According to Jiang Feng, in an email to the author, "In Pinyin, Emily Dickinson's name is Aimili Dijinsen, six syllables: Ai-mi-li Di-jin-sen. *Dijinsen*, its Chinese pronunciation is most similar to that of *Dickinson*, because there isn't a word sounding *kin* or *king* in Chinese language. The first Sino-gram *Di*, is a character always used as name of a tribe or family, the *jin* means gold, and *sen* means forest. In Chinese, every gram has its own meaning; *Dijinsen* means Gold Forest of Di, the family or tribe.

The sound of *Amili* is completely equivalent to Emily. *Ai* is a fragrant grass, *mi* is rice, *li*, jasmine, always selected as name for girls.

Before this name translation, she was named Di Gengsheng in the Foreign Literature volume of a Chinese Encyclopedia. But the name I gave has been accepted by readers and scholars since it appeared with the Chinese version of her five poems, published in *Poetry*."

50 *I felt the same*   For Feng's translations of Shelley and Emily Dickinson and many other poets, he won China's first ever prize for lifetime achievement for literary translation, when he was sixty years old. Today, he is known as well for his theory of literary translation: "Similarity implies fidelity." I fulfilled my vow to him in the fall of 2008. Feng visited his daughter, a software engineer in California, then flew to Amherst to speak at a forum on language and translation, then to Minneapolis. After attending a reading by poet/translators Robert Bly and Robert Hedin in Red Wing, Minnesota, we rode the train to Chicago to visit the Poetry Foundation, publisher of *Poetry* magazine. I was not surprised that he knew all about *Poetry* and its intrepid founder, Harriet Monroe, who first published Ezra Pound's Chinese-style verses and Arthur Waley's translations.

50 *Weave a circle*   Coleridge, *The Complete Poetical Works*, 298.

CHAPTER NINE

53 *In his essay*   Robert Bly, "Six Disciplines That Intensify Poetry," *The Thousands: A Magazine of Poetry and General Opinion*, 2001, 10.

53 *According to his best translator*   Mike O'Connor, *When I Find You Again It Will Be in Mountains: Selected Poems of Chia Tao* (Somerville, MA: Wisdom Publications, 2000), 4.

54 *Morning Travel*   Ibid., 17.

CHAPTER TEN

63 *Abbott Minghai once said*   Quoted by Bill Porter, *Zen Baggage: A Pilgrimage to China* (Berkeley: Counterpoint, 2009), 107.

CHAPTER ELEVEN

66 *The Master said*   Confucius, *The Analects of Confucius*, trans. Arthur Waley (New York: Vintage, 1989), 212.

67 *According to Eliot Weinberger*   Eliot Weinberger, ed., *The New Directions Anthology of Classical Chinese Poetry* (New York: New Directions, 2003), xix.

67 *By the time I was sixteen*   W. S. Merwin, *East Window: The Asian Translations* (Port Townsend, WA: Copper Canyon Press, 1998), 3.

68 *Our aim was to bring*   "A Couple of Literary Outlaws: An Interview with Robert Bly and William Duffy on the Founding of *The Fifties*," *Great River Review*, Fall/Winter 1998, 48-49.

68 *Collect from deep thoughts*   Lu Chi, *Lu Chi's Wen Fu: The Art of Writing*, trans. Sam Hamill (Minneapolis: Milkweed Editions, 1991), 11.

CHAPTER TWELVE

73 *The fish trap exists*   Zhuangzi, *Zhuangzi: Basic Writings*, trans. Burton Watson (New York: Columbia University Press, 2003), 141.

73 *According to Burton Watson*   Ibid., 5.

76 *Sitting Alone on Chingting Mountain*   Li Pai [Li Bai], *Poems of the Masters: China's Classic Anthology of T'ang and Sung Dynasty Verse*, trans. Red Pine [Bill Porter] (Port Townsend, WA: Copper Canyon Press, 2003), 17.

76 *Recording My Thoughts*   Tu Fu [Du Fu], *Poems of the Masters*, 135.

77 *Bill's hardy North American namesake*   In later correspondence, Bill told the author that Sheng-yun, "Victorious Cloud," was his name

at Fokuangshan Monastery in Taiwan where he lived from 1972 to 1973, and at Haiming Monastery, where he lived from 1974 to 1976. That name was given by Master Shou-yeh in 1971 during Zen training in New York after Bill finished studies in Chinese and anthropology at Columbia. "That's me," laughed Bill, "cloudy but victorious."

CHAPTER THIRTEEN

80 *On the Birth of His Son*   Su Dongpo, *Translations from the Chinese*, trans. Arthur Waley (New York: Knopf, 1919), 324.

81 *Spring Night*   Su Shih [Su Dongpo], *Poems of the Masters*, 185.

81 *Flower Shadows*   Ibid., 245.

84 *"Seeing your nature is Zen"*   *The Zen Teachings of Bodhidharma*, trans. Red Pine [Bill Porter] (New York: North Point Press, 1987), xv.

CHAPTER FOURTEEN

85 *the greatest non-epic*   Kenneth Roxroth, *One Hundred Poems from the Chinese* (New York: New Directions, 1971), 135. San Francisco poet and translator Kenneth Rexroth loved Du Fu the way I love Hanshan. In 1971, he wrote in *One Hundred Poems from the Chinese:* "I have had the work of Tu Fu [Du Fu] by me since adolescence and over the years have come to know these poems better than most of my own. . . . I have thought of my translations as, finally, expressions of myself."

86 *The tomb said to hold his body*   Tu Fu [Du Fu], *The Selected Poems of Du Fu*, trans. Burton Watson (New York: Columbia University Press, 2002), xvi.

86 *To Pi Ssu Yao*   Tu Fu [Du Fu], *The New Directions Anthology of Classical Chinese Poetry*, trans. Kenneth Rexroth (New York: New Directions, 2003), 108.

87 *Song of the War-Carts*   Tu Fu [Du Fu], *The New Directions Anthology*, trans. David Hinton, 97.

89 *Snow Storm*   Du Fu, *The New Directions Anthology*, trans. Kenneth Rexroth, 98.

90 *At the Vietnam Memorial*   James P. Lenfestey, *A Cartload of Scrolls* (Duluth, MN: Holy Cow! Press, 2007), 36.

90 *Driving Across Wisconsin*   James P. Lenfestey, *Saying Grace* (Marshfield, WI: Marsh River Editions, 2004), 15.

Chapter Fifteen

93 *We rode a motorboat shuttle*   Burton Watson, ed., *The Columbia Book of Chinese Poetry*, 242.

94 *Idle Droning*   Bai Juyi, *The Columbia Book of Chinese Poetry*, trans. Burton Watson, 256.

Chapter Sixteen

98 *Therefore the sage goes*   Lao Tsu [Laozi], *Tao Te Ching*, trans. Gia-Fu Feng and Jane English (New York: Vintage, 1972).

99 *The Tao that can be told*   Ibid.

Chapter Seventeen

102 *Climate Change*   Lenfestey, *A Cartload of Scrolls*, 92.

Chapter Eighteen

106 *Steve and I left the Sian*   Bill Porter, *Road to Heaven: Encounters with Chinese Hermits,* (Berkeley, CA: Counterpoint Press, 2009).

107 *Throughout Chinese history*   Ibid., I.

Chapter Nineteen

109 *Poem by Wang Wei*   Ibid., 204

Chapter Twenty

118 *Cold Mountain no. 39*   Han-shan, *Cold Mountain: 100 Poems*, 57.

118 *The Lake Isle of Innisfree*   William Butler Yeats, *The Collected Peoms of W.B. Yeats*, ed. Richard J. Finneran (New York: Simon & Schuster, 1983), 39.

119 *Inversnaid*   Gerard Manley Hopkins, *Gerard Manley Hopkins: Poems and Prose* (New York: Penguin, 1953), 50.

120 *Waking Up*   Robert Bly, *A Private Fall* (Minneapolis: Melia Press, 1995).

121 *Under the pines*   Chia Tao [Jia Dao], *The Columbia Book of Chinese Poetry*, 285.

Chapter Twenty-One

124 *I recalled the poet Charles Wright*   Adapted from *Charles Wright & Adrienne Rich* (New York: Academy of American Poets, 1997), Track 15, Disc I. Audio recording on CD.

Chapter Twenty-Three

134 *Thoughts on a Quiet Night*   Li Pai [Li Bai], *Poems of the Masters*, 65.

134 *Love Poem*   Thorsten Bacon, originally published as a broadside (Ojai, CA: TreeHouse Press, 2006).

135 *How could I have come*   Thomas McGrath, *Letters to Tomasito*, (Minneapolis: Holy Cow! Press, 1977), 14.

135 *As he once wrote*   Paul Hansen, *Before Ten Thousand Peaks: Poems from the Chinese* (Port Townsend, WA: Copper Canyon Press, 1980), 17.

135 *The Art of Literary Translation*   Sam Hamill [Obaka-san the Pilgrim, pseud.]. Text taken from a printed bookmark.

CHAPTER TWENTY-FOUR

138 *Drinking Alone with the Moon*   Li Po [Li Bai], *Endless River: Li Po and Tu Fu: A Friendship in Poetry*, trans. Sam Hamill (New York: Weatherhill, 1993).

140 *Traveling Away from Home*   Li Pai [Li Bai], *Poems of the Masters*, 231.

140 *Seeing Off a Friend*   Ibid., 101.

CHAPTER TWENTY-FIVE

142 *Cold Mountain no. 80*   Han-shan, *Cold Mountain: 100 Poems*, 98.

CHAPTER TWENTY-SIX

145 *Thousands of feet high*   Li Bai, trans. unknown. http://www.thingsasian.com/stories-photos/2496

CHAPTER TWENTY-SEVEN

151 *without doubt the finest*   Marco Polo, *The Travels of Marco Polo*, trans. Ronald Latham (New York: Abaris Books, Inc., 1982), 184.

153 *Drinking on the Lake*   Su Shih [Su Dongpo], *Poems of the Masters*, 327.

154 *The shining city*   William Ellery Leonard, *Two Lives: A Poem* (New York: B.W. Huebsch, Inc., 1925).

155 *Courage at Sixty*   Eugene J. McCarthy, *Selected Poems* (Rochester, MN: Lone Oak Press, 1997), 71.

CHAPTER TWENTY-NINE

161 *Cold Mountain no. 38*   Han-shan, *Cold Mountain: 100 Poems*, 56.

162 *Watson wrote in a note*   Burton Watson, *Cold Mountain: 100 Poems*, 56.

163 *Cold Mountain no. 1*   Han-shan, *Cold Mountain: 100 Poems*, 19.

CHAPTER THIRTY

165 *Wonderful, this road to Cold Mountain*   Ibid., 66.

CHAPTER THIRTY-ONE

174 *A blind boy aiming*   Ibid, 37.

176 *Once in the Sixties*   Inspired by William Stafford's "Once in the Forties"

177 *I Am Not I*   Juan Ramón Jiménez, *Lorca and Jiménez*, trans. Robert Bly (Boston: Beacon Press, 1973), 77.

178 *My Father*   James P. Lenfestey, *Into the Goodhue County Jail: Poems to Free Prisoners* (Red Wing, MN: Red Dragonfly Press, 2008), 25.

179 *Glacial Erratic*   Lenfestey, *A Cartload of Scrolls*, 105.

181 *Steady Work*   Lenfestey, *Into the Goodhue County Jail*, 33.

CHAPTER THIRTY-TWO

183 *Now it is that*   Han-shan, *Cold Mountain: 100 Poems*, 66.

185 *The packer saw Han-shan*   Snyder, *Riprap and Cold Mountain Poems*, 35.

CHAPTER THIRTY-THREE

187 *I ordered Tao-ch'iao*   Ibid.

188 *the poems in this book*   Waley, *Translations from the Chinese*, preface.

CHAPTER THIRTY-FOUR

189 *Now I face home again*   Walt Whitman, *Leaves of Grass* (1867; Project Gutenberg, 2008). http://www.gutenberg.org/files/1322/1322-h/1322-h.htm#link2H_4_0042

POSTSCRIPT

195 *Drink, Pilgrim, here!*   Samuel Taylor Coleridge, *The Complete Poetical Works of Samuel Taylor Coleridge*, ed. Ernest Hartley Coleridge (Oxford: Oxford at the Clarendon Press, 1912; Project Gutenberg, 2009), 382. http://www.gutenberg.org/files/29090/29090-h/29090-h.htm

CODA

TEXT FOR A CARVED STONE STELA
TO BE PLACED NEAR
COLD MOUNTAIN'S CAVE

Five pilgrims from America ascended
peaks and descended elevators
exploring poetry, Buddhism, and history
in the autumn of 2006.
Stories of their wine drinking linger
throughout the country, and in their minds.
At Han-shan's cave, they were briefly still.
Ask the current hermit if you don't believe.

POEMS AND TEXT USED BY PERMISSION

LIST OF SOURCES

Bashō, Matsuo. *The Narrow Road to the Deep North and Other Travel Sketches.* Translated by Nobuyuki Yuasa. New York: Penguin Classics, 1966. This book led me down the haibun road. It includes as well *Records of a Weather-Exposed Skeleton* and *The Records of a Travel-Worn Satchel.*

Bly, Robert. "Six Disciplines That Intensify Poetry." *The Thousands: A Magazine of Poetry and General Opinion.* Minneapolis: The Thousands Press, 2001.

Bodhidharma. *The Zen Teachings of Bodhidharma.* Translated by Red Pine. New York: North Point Press, 1989.

Cai, Zong-qi, ed. *How to Read Chinese Poetry: A Guided Anthology.* New York: Columbia University Press, 2008. A very useful tool I encountered in the library of Poet's House in New York late in the process of this book. Full of clear explanations of poetry mechanics, especially helpful on the *lü-shih*, "undoubtedly one of the most complicated kinds of poetry in the world . . . a poet must strictly follow complex, interlocked sets of rules for word choice, syntax, structure, and tonal patterning" (161).

Chia Tao. *When I Find You Again It Will Be in Mountains: Selected Poems of Chia Tao.* Translated by Mike O'Connor. Somerville, MA: Wisdom Publications, 2000.

Chung, Ling. "Canonization of Han Shan's Poetry in the West, 1950–2000." Unpublished paper, private communication. Ling directly pursues the astonishment of the Chinese that Cold Mountain, "who for a millennium had never been accepted by the Chinese literati as a serious poet," aroused interest in the West, particularly America. She traces his "canonization" to Snyder's translations, which were included in Cyril Birch's 1965 *Anthology of Chinese Literature,* and to Jack Kerouac's idolization of both Snyder and Han-shan in *The Dharma Bums.* In this version of the paper she never significantly considers any influence by Burton Watson's paperback 1970 *Cold Mountain* collection.

Chuang Tsu. *Chuang Tsu: Inner Chapters.* Translated by Gia-Fu Feng and Jane English. New York: Vintage Books, 1974.

Confucius. *The Analects of Confucius*. Translated by Arthur Waley. New York: Vintage Books, 1989.

Confucius. *The Analects of Confucius*. Translated by Burton Watson. New York: Columbia University Press, 2007. A new translation. Wonderfully readable, like Waley's, Watson's scholarship is helpful yet never intrusive.

Du Fu. *The Selected Poems of Du Fu*. Translated by Burton Watson. New York: Columbia University Press, 2002.

Hamill, Sam, and J. P. Seaton, translators and editors. *The Poetry of Zen*. Boston: Shambhala, 2004. A "must" for every backpack.

Hansen, Paul. *Before Ten Thousand Peaks: Translations from the Chinese*. Port Townsend, WA: Copper Canyon Press, 1980. A valuable introduction.

Han-shan. *The Poetry of Han-shan: A Complete, Annotated Translation of Cold Mountain*. Translated by Robert G. Henricks. New York: State University of New York Press, 1990. Henricks extensively footnotes the poems, and is especially good on their multiple Zen possibilities. His edition, although earlier than Red Pine's, reached me well after *Collected Songs of Cold Mountain*. A worthy scholarly companion, though Henricks's adverbial translations are off-putting to this poet. But the scholarship is rich and rewarding. Who would have thought this mysterious laughing recluse would become not only a bodhisattva but a full plate for scholars' knives and forks?

Han-shan. *The Collected Songs of Cold Mountain*. Translated by Red Pine (Bill Porter). Port Townsend, WA: Copper Canyon Press, 2000. The photo of the cave set me on the actual road to Cold Mountain. In this bilingual edition, Porter's scholarship and geographical knowledge are without peer, and the introduction by reclusive scholar John Blofeld is mind-blowing. For his translations, Porter made the decision to follow Chinese convention and forgo capital letters and punctuation, which can make some of them a bit hard to follow.

Han-shan. *Cold Mountain: 100 Poems by the T'ang Poet Han-shan*. Translated by Burton Watson. New York: Grove Press, 1962; New York: Columbia University Press, 1970. Watson's incomparable edition that started it all, his brilliantly musical translations usefully arranged in biographical order deduced from evidence in the poems. I carry it with me everywhere, some of the poems memorized.

SEEKING THE CAVE

Hinton, David. *Mountain Home: The Wilderness Poetry of Ancient China*. Berkeley: Counterpoint, 2002. Superb translations and introduction illuminating the important concept of *tzu-jan*, "self-ablaze."

Holm, Bill. *Coming Home Crazy: An Alphabet of China Essays*. Minneapolis: Milkweed Editions, 2000. My poet friend Bill's hilarious adventures and misadventures teaching English in Xi'an in the late eighties.

Lao Tsu. *Tao Te Ching*. Translated by Gia-Fu Feng and Jane English. New York: Vintage Books, 1972. Both this and their *Chuang Tsu* are elegantly designed with floating-world photographs and poetic translations.

Li Po and Tu Fu. *Endless River: Li Po and Tu Fu: A Friendship in Poetry*. Translated by Sam Hamill. New York: Weatherhill, 1993.

Li Po and Tu Fu. *Li Po and Tu Fu: Poems*. Translated by Arthur Cooper. London: Penguin Classics, 1973. Cooper, a retired British civil servant once stationed in Hong Kong, bucked the twentieth-century trend by translating the poems musically, to wonderful effect. One can almost sing them, or accompany them on a lute, the way they were originally performed.

Lu Chi. *Lu Chi's Wen Fu: The Art of Writing*. Translated by Sam Hamill. Minneapolis: Milkweed Editions, 2000. A "must" for every writer's backpack.

MacKinnon, John, and Karen Phillipps. *A Field Guide to the Birds of China*. Oxford and New York: Oxford University Press, 2000. The brick I hauled around China with little need, but happy I had it.

O'Connor, Mike, and Red Pine (Bill Porter), editors. *The Clouds Should Know Me by Now: Buddhist Poet Monks of China*. Somerville, MA: Wisdom Publications, 1998. Translations by Paul Hansen, Red Pine, James Sanford, J. P. Seaton, and Burton Watson.

Owen, Stephen, editor and translator. *An Anthology of Chinese Literature: Beginnings to 1911*. New York: W. W. Norton, 1996. From "A Note on Translation": for the scholar, translation is "a troubling art. . . . It is literary history gone gambling. . . an enterprise where luck rules." Some fine translations too.

Payne, Robert, editor. *The White Pony: An Anthology of Chinese Poetry from the Earliest Times to the Present Day*. London: Allen and Unwin, 1949. Fine translations (by Payne and numerous others) that inspired Robert Bly, James Wright, and others in the second half of the twentieth century.

Poems of the Masters: China's Classic Anthology of T'ang and Sung Dynasty Verse. Translated by Red Pine (Bill Porter). Washington: Copper Canyon Press, 2003. A bilingual edition with invaluable scholarly and geographic notes.

Porter, Bill. *Road to Heaven: Encounters with Chinese Hermits.* Berkeley: Counterpoint, 1993, 2009. There is nothing like Bill's hermit-hunting ramble, and nothing like this book, a classic.

Porter, Bill. *Zen Baggage: A Pilgrimage to China.* Berkeley: Counterpoint, 2009. Bill's own mountain road: unbelievable and true.

Rexroth, Kenneth. *One Hundred Poems from the Chinese.* New York: New Directions, 1971. I think of Rexroth's translations more as versions because Rexroth "translates" as he pleases, fine to read.

Rexroth, Kenneth. *One Hundred More Poems from the Chinese: Love and the Turning Year.* New York: New Directions, 1971.

Ryōkan. *Ryōkan: Zen Monk-Poet of Japan.* Translated by Burton Watson. New York: Columbia University Press, 1977. The Japanese poet-eccentric who also claimed Cold Mountain as his teacher.

Snyder, Gary. *Riprap and Cold Mountain Poems.* Berkeley: Counterpoint, 2010; Four Seasons Foundation, 1958. Includes the only complete translation of the preface by Lü Ch'iu-Yin to the original Han-shan collection, plus twenty-four superb if idiosyncratic translations first published in *Evergreen Review* No. 6, 1958. These translations, undertaken when Snyder was a graduate student in Asian languages at Berkeley, famously influenced his visitors Allen Ginsberg and Jack Kerouac, who dedicated his 1958 novel *The Dharma Bums* to Han-shan.

Su Tung-p'o. *Selected Poems of Su Tung-p'o.* Translated by Burton Watson. Port Townsend, WA: Copper Canyon Press, 1994.

Waley, Arthur, with illustrations by Cyrus Leroy Baldridge. *Translations from the Chinese.* New York: Alfred A. Knopf, 1940. The only home I know of for the Su Dongpo poem "On the Birth of His Son." Where Bill Holm found it, and I memorized it.

Waley, Arthur. *Arthur Waley's Chinese Poems.* London: Unwin Books, 1961. I haven't been able to find a copy, but, according to Burton Watson, it contains the twenty-seven Han-shan translations first published in *Encounter* in 1954.

Watson, Burton. *Chinese Lyricism: Shih Poetry from the Second to the Twelfth Century.* New York: Columbia University Press, 1971. Extremely helpful for lay readers attempting to sort out the variety of Chinese poetic forms, particularly the *shih* used by Han-shan and others in the T'ang and Song. I still have a very long way to go to understand the forms, no fault of Watson's impeccable effort here. I absorbed the rhythm of his Han-shan translations through osmosis over thirty years.

Watson, Burton, editor and translator. *The Columbia Book of Chinese Poetry: From Early Times to the Thirteenth Century.* New York: Columbia University Press, 1984. This is the textbook known by students of Chinese literature, but new to me in the months before my departure. Indispensable.

Watson, Burton. *Four Huts: Asian Writings on the Simple Life.* Boston: Shambhala, 2002. Four prose texts by real or wannabe recluses: *Record of the Thatched Hall on Mount Lu* by Po Chü-i; *Record of the Pond Pavilion* by Yoshishige no Yasutane; *Record of the Ten-Foot-Square Hut* by Kamo no Chōmei; *Record of the Hut of the Phantom Dwelling* by Matsuo Bashō.

Weinberger, Eliot, editor. *The New Directions Anthology of Classical Chinese Poetry.* New York: New Directions, 2003. Do not miss Weinberger's important introductory essay on the transformative influence of translated Chinese poetry on twentieth-century American poetry.

Zhuangzi. *Zhuangzi: Basic Writings.* Translated by Burton Watson. New York: Columbia University Press, 2003.

ACKNOWLEDGMENTS

The following poems and prose were previously published, sometimes in earlier forms, in the following publications.

"Homeless Dogs," "Setting Lead Type," "At the Vietnam Memorial," "Climate Change," "Glacial Erratic" in *A Cartload Of Scrolls: 100 Poems in the Manner of T'ang Dynasty Poet Han-shan* (Duluth: Holy Cow! Press, 2006).

"Driving Across Wisconsin, September 11, 2001," in *Saying Grace* (Marshfield, WI: Marsh River Editions, 2002).

"Bug in a Pool" in *Margie: The American Journal of Poetry.*

"My Father" and "Steady Work" in *Into the Goodhue County Jail: Poems to Free Prisoners* (Northfield, MN: Red Dragonfly Press, 2007).

"Encounter with the Arch-Translator" in *POIESIS* 12.

"Wang Wei's Advice," in *The Kerf.*

"Moon Music" in *POIESIS* 13.

JAMES P. LENFESTEY is a former college English instructor, alternative school administrator, marketing communications consultant, and editorial writer for the *Star Tribune*, where he won several Page One awards for excellence. Since 2000, he has published a collection of essays, a poetry anthology, five collections of his own poems, several poetry chapbooks, and co-edited *Robert Bly in This World* (University of Minnesota Press). As a journalist he covers education, energy policy, and climate science. He lives in Minneapolis with his wife of forty-seven years. They have four children and seven grandchildren.

INTERIOR DESIGN & TYPESETTING BY

MARY AUSTIN SPEAKER

Typeset in Centaur

Centaur was drawn as titling capitals for a book about the mythical creature of the same name in 1914 by renowned classical typographer Bruce Rogers for the Metropolitan Museum of Art. Rogers' design for the typeface was influenced by such fifteenth century texts as Nicholas Jenson's *Eusebius* and Pietro Bembo's *De Aetna*. The metal typeface was privately cast by the American Type Foundry and released by the Monotype Corporation in 1929.

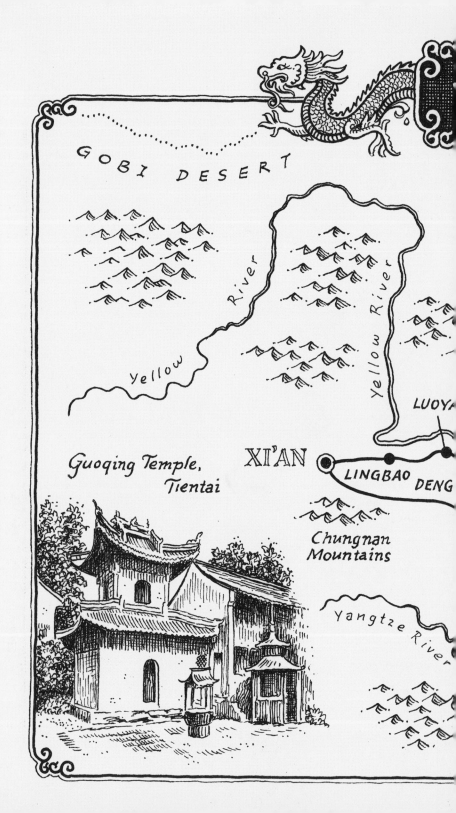

GOBI DESERT

Yellow River

Yellow River

LUOYA

XI'AN

Guoqing Temple, Tientai

LINGBAO DENG

Chungnan Mountains

Yangtze River